Occasional Paper No. 47

Aging and Social Expenditure in the Major Industrial Countries, 1980-2025

By Peter S. Heller, Richard Hemming, and Peter W. Kohnert,

with a staff team consisting of

Robert Alan Feldman
Menachem Katz
Ahsan Mansur
Donogh McDonald
Bernard Nivollet
Edoardo Ruggiero
Ziba Farhadian

International Monetary Fund
Washington, D.C.
September 1986

Library of Congress Cataloging-in-Publication Data

Heller, Peter S.
Aging and social expenditure in the major industrial countries, 1980–2025.

(Occasional paper, ISSN 0251-6365 ; no. 47)
Bibliography: p.
1. Expenditures, Public. 2. Expenditures, Public—Forecasting. 3. Social policy. 4. Age distribution (Demography) I. Hemming, Richard. II. Kohnert, Peter. III. Feldman, Robert Alan. IV. Title. V. Series: Occasional paper (International Monetary Fund) ; no. 47.
HJ7469.H45 1986 336.3'9 86-20835
ISBN 0-939934-68-X

Price: US$7.50
(US$4.50 university libraries, faculty members, and students)

Address orders to:
External Relations Department, Publications Unit
International Monetary Fund, Washington, D.C. 20431

Contents

CHARTS

The following symbols have been used throughout this paper:

. . . to indicate that data are not available;

— to indicate that the figure is zero or less than half the final digit shown, or that the item does not exist;

– between years or months (e.g., 1979–81 or January–June) to indicate the years or months covered, including the beginning and ending years or months;

/ between years (e.g., 1980/81) to indicate a crop or fiscal (financial) year.

"Billion" means a thousand million.

Minor discrepancies between constituent figures and totals are due to rounding.

Preface

In early 1984, several members of the Fund's Executive Board proposed that the Fiscal Affairs Department of the Fund conduct a comparative study of trends in government social expenditures, with particular attention to the implications of demographic trends in the industrial countries. A number of issues were of particular interest. What was likely to be the impact of the aging of the populations of the industrial countries on their outlays for social expenditures? Would diminished outlays for education offset increased outlays for pensions and medical care and what would be the impact on the share of social outlays in total output? What was the likely time pattern of evolution of social expenditures and would this be a significant factor to consider in the formulation of fiscal policy in the present? At the same time, the Organization for Economic Cooperation and Development (OECD) was in the process of completing a report that examined the factors underlying the evolution of social expenditures since 1960 in the OECD countries, with projections on the likely growth of social expenditure through 1990. The Fund study can be viewed as a complement to the OECD report, as it evaluates the impact of current demographic trends over the longer time frame during which the demographic structure will most demonstrably change. The focus is limited to the seven major industrial countries.

Given the significant differences that exist across countries in their social programs, seven individual country studies were made, providing detailed demographic and expenditure projections through the year 2025. Each of the countries generously provided assistance, both in the form of data and in commenting on drafts of the individual country studies. To obtain information and collect views for these papers, the staff held discussions with authorities in Bonn, London, Ottawa, Paris, Rome, Tokyo, and Washington. Officials of the OECD provided data and advice on many of the problems involved in the analysis and projection of social expenditures. Under the direction of Peter S. Heller, Chief, Government Expenditure Analysis Division of the Fiscal Affairs Department, the seven studies were carried out by Robert Alan Feldman, Menachem Katz, Peter W. Kohnert, Ahsan Mansur, Donogh McDonald, Bernard Nivollet (all members of the Fiscal Affairs Department), and Edgardo Ruggiero, a consultant. A cross-country analysis of education expenditure was also carried out by Ziba Farhadian of the Fiscal Affairs Department.

On the basis of these papers, this report was prepared by Mr. Heller, in collaboration with Richard Hemming and Mr. Kohnert of the Fiscal Affairs Department. In general, the results correspond to those in the individual country studies. In some cases, the earlier analyses were modified to ensure greater comparability in either the classification of particular expenditure categories or in the particular economic or demographic assumptions. While the study also attempts to incorporate the impact of the most recent policy measures, the paper reflects data available prior to June 1985.

In analyzing the results of this study several words of caution should be emphasized. First, there remain considerable differences across countries, both in terms of their definition of what is included in ''government social expenditure'' and in the relative importance of the private and public sectors in the provision and financing of social programs. For example, the private sector is extremely important in the financing of pensions in such countries as the United States, Canada, and Japan, whereas in others, such as the Federal Republic of Germany and France, the private sector's role is limited. In the former countries, emphasis on the growth in the government's social expenditure will significantly understate the overall resource allocational implications of the growth in the share of the elderly in the population. Consequently, more emphasis should be placed on the trends in expenditure for a *country over time* than differences in the ratio of expenditure to GDP *across countries at any point in time*.

Second, one should stress the inherent dangers in any projections extending 45 years into the future. The results are highly sensitive to the assumptions on the economic and demographic parameters and the fairly restrictive assumptions embodied in the specification of the projection model. In some areas of social expenditure, the projections are inherently more uncertain than in others. Projections that depend on forecasts of the birth rate (e.g., education) are much more uncertain than those depending on forecasts of the death rate. Similarly, the projections are particularly sensitive to the assumptions made on the likely growth of real pension benefits and on the real cost of medical and educational services. In specifying the model, it is also difficult to fully incorporate the inevitable linkages that will exist between a shrinking working-age population (such as in the Federal Republic of Germany) and the rate of labor force participation and unemployment. One also can expect that policy responses, if not already emerging, will take place to counter some of the trends implied in these projections.

Finally, it should be emphasized that the results presented in this study are *projections* not predictions. They cannot be seen as realistic forecasts of future developments that might be considered as probable. If social expenditures were to increase as suggested by the projections, this would threaten, if not put in jeopardy, the ability of the economy to cope with the problem of intergenerational equity in a context of steady economic growth. Thus, it would be quite surprising if the legislation pertaining to social expenditure were to remain unchanged until the year 2025. In fact, many countries have already initiated measures for adjustment in a medium-term framework, recognizing the long lead time necessary to affect expenditure in some sectors. In addition to such measures, it is to be expected that the need to develop long-term policies for strengthening productivity will gain increasing attention, not least with a view to securing the ability of social expenditure systems to cope with the challenge of an increasing burden on the active part of the population.

The authors have benefited from helpful comments by staff in the Fiscal Affairs Department and other departments of the Fund and by members of the Executive Board. However, the opinions expressed are those of the authors and do not necessarily represent the views of other staff members or of Executive Directors. Research assistance was provided by Tarja Papavassiliou. The authors are particularly indebted to the secretarial efforts of Anamaría Handford, Gail Hinds, Nita Merchant, and Marion Jacobson. The authors also wish to thank the editor, Ella Wright.

I Evolution of Social Expenditure in the Group of Seven Major Industrial Countries, 1980–2025

Introduction

Most of the seven major industrial countries are now experiencing significant changes in their demographic structure. A persistent pattern of declining fertility and improving life expectancy has created major segments of the population that are already relatively aged or will become so in the near future. This substantial change in the demographic structure is likely to have far-reaching implications. As to the economic ramifications alone, it is likely to affect the size, structure, and dynamics of the labor force and may cause difficulties in accommodating an aging work force; it may significantly challenge the maintenance of sustained and buoyant growth; and it is likely to alter the demand for goods and services. As to implications for the public sector, it is likely to influence the demand not only for pensions, but for other social expenditures as well (on education, medical care, etc.). Furthermore, such a change could pose serious financial problems as the working-age segment of the population shrinks in proportion to the retired segment, heightening the likelihood of intergenerational conflict. In most countries, concern over the aging problem has led to considerable discussion and the enactment of specific policy measures in the areas of pensions and medical care. Nevertheless, despite the potential importance of this issue, none of the seven major industrial countries has undertaken a comprehensive analysis of the combined impact of an aging population on the various components of government expenditure.[1]

While the Fund has often been accused of dealing only with short-term aspects of the economy, its function of surveillance clearly extends to evaluating whether short- and medium-term policies should be influenced by long-term structural developments. Long-term demographic changes are clearly of this nature, signaling the need for anticipatory policy measures while potentially constraining current policy options. Such concerns led several Executive Directors in early 1984 to suggest that the Fiscal Affairs Department conduct a comparative study of trends in government social expenditure in the industrial countries, with particular attention to the implications of current demographic trends.

This paper examines the impact of prospective demographic trends on the level and structure of social expenditure by the governments of the seven major industrial countries (the Group of Seven) through the year 2025. It attempts to place these demographic factors in perspective with the other factors likely to influence the growth of social expenditure. It also reviews the key policy issues likely to emerge, both at an aggregate and a sectoral level, and the types of policies countries have initiated in trying to cope with the effects of these demographic trends.[2]

The focus is on government expenditure in the different social sectors. Social expenditure is defined to include, as a central core, medical care, education, pensions, welfare payments, unemployment insurance, and family benefits. A smaller residual category of social expenditure is included which differs across countries (see Chapter II). No change in the existing division of responsibility between the public and private sectors is assumed for any social program, nor is any evaluation made as to whether such changes would be more efficient in meeting given social objectives.

[1] Most studies in the Group of Seven industrial countries have focused on the effects of aging on the pension system and occasionally on the cost of medical insurance programs. Studies on the evolution of total social expenditure have been undertaken in some of the smaller industrial countries (e.g., Australia: Social Welfare Policy Secretariat (1984); the Netherlands: Goudriaan and others (1984); and Ireland: National Economic and Social Council (1984). Also, see Rosa (1982) and United Kingdom (1985).

[2] This is not only an industrial country problem. It may also emerge in developing countries seeking to limit their population growth. A recent article in the *China Daily* (''Opinion: An Appeal to Revise Old Age Insurance'' (1985)) notes that the proportion of China's population in the age group 60 and over is expected to double every 30 years, reaching 15 percent by 2010 and 30 percent by 2040. ''The proportion of the retired population . . . to the labouring population was 14 percent in 1980. It . . . will reach 19 percent in 2000 and even as high as 54 percent by 2040.''

Similarly, no attempt is made to provide a detailed examination of the financial viability of particular social programs, nor to speculate on the sources of financing that might be required to fill potential resource gaps. Neither is there an attempt to quantify the shift in the balance of overall demand for resources by the young, the working-age, and the elderly populations, as this will be influenced by the relative importance of the private sector in a given country in providing for the needs of the elderly and those of the young.

This paper is based on the results of detailed studies by the Fund's Fiscal Affairs Department on the probable evolution of government social expenditure in each of the seven major industrial countries.[3] While similar in overall design and methodology, the individual country studies were carried out independently, with the intention of accurately reflecting national views on the development of key demographic and economic parameters, the scale of existing social expenditure programs, and the factors likely to influence their evolution. In those studies, the specific national definitions of expenditure in any given social sector were used.

In this paper, some attempt has been made to eliminate areas of sharp incomparability, both in the definition of social expenditure categories and in specific assumptions on parameters, and to explain the factors underlying major differences in the size and structure of particular expenditure programs across countries. In addition, this paper seeks to incorporate the impact of recent policy developments, especially with respect to pensions, and to adjust the projections for the effect of any significant changes in the social expenditure base between 1980 and the present. Nevertheless, on balance the results largely reflect those of the individual country studies, and more emphasis should be placed on an examination of the trends in expenditure for a given country over time than on an excessive focus on the differences in the ratio of expenditure to gross domestic product (GDP) across countries at any given point in time.[4]

It should be emphasized that the results presented are projections, *not* predictions. While projections of the population structure for 20–25 years in the future have a reasonably high degree of credibility, beyond this time frame increasing uncertainty must inevitably be attached to the results. By evaluating the impact of alternative demographic scenarios, this study has attempted to capture the range of possible outcomes. Nevertheless, one should recognize the limits of this type of analysis. Equally relevant, though based on reasonable assumptions, many outcomes appear to be politically unsustainable, particularly when judged by the financing burdens that they would imply. Such results effectively signal the need for, and the likelihood of, changes in the institutions, procedures, real benefit levels, and policies associated with important social services and transfers. Equally likely, the projected demographic shifts could themselves induce reactions in the economy that are at least partially corrective. For example, the increased demands of an enlarged elderly component of the population are likely to create labor market pressures to keep more of the elderly in active employment beyond the (heretofore) "normal retirement age."

Such changes, only some of which are immediately foreseeable, would almost certainly alleviate some of the financial burdens implied by the projections. Certainly in the area of pensions and medical care, considerable thought is being given in most of the seven countries to ways in which to stem the anticipated growth in expenditures, and this is being translated into concrete policy measures. The recent pension reform measures in Japan, the Federal Republic of Germany, the United Kingdom, and the United States, and the policies instituted to control medical costs in the United States and other countries are manifestations of these efforts. In fact, in some countries, the appearance of sustainability in the projections for some programs may be the *result* of the implementation of such recent policy measures specifically designed to address the rising financial burden associated with the aging of the population. In cases where the results are not sustainable, it is hoped that this study will help to signal the need for changes in social service and transfer programs.

The remainder of this chapter summarizes the principal results for each of the seven major industrial

[3] As a survey paper, this study will not provide detailed institutional descriptions of the individual countries. Such discussions are presented in the following country studies by Fund staff members:

Robert Alan Feldman, "Japan: Outlook for Social Expenditure, 1980–2025" (unpublished, July 1985).

Menachem Katz, "The Future of Expenditure on Social Programs in Canada, 1980–2025" (unpublished, August 1985).

Peter Kohnert, "Social Expenditure Developments in the Federal Republic of Germany, 1980–2025" (unpublished, August 1985).

Ahsan Mansur, "United Kingdom: Developments in Public Social Expenditure, 1980–2025" (unpublished, July 1985).

Donogh McDonald, "United States: Outlook for Social Expenditure, 1980–2025" (unpublished, August 1985).

Bernard Nivollet, "Scenarios on Social Expenditure Trends in France, 1980–2025" (unpublished, July 1985).

Edgardo Ruggiero, "Social Expenditure Developments in Italy, 1980–2025" (unpublished, July 1985).

See also Ziba Farhadian, "Public Expenditure on Education" (unpublished, February 1985), for details on the education sector.

[4] Several of the countries in this study use gross national product (GNP) as the principal measure of output (notably Canada, the Federal Republic of Germany, the United Kingdom, and the United States). In this study, all ratios to output for these countries have been calculated and expressed in the tables with respect to GNP. However, GDP is the term used in the text for references to total output.

countries, with emphasis on the probable trend of the ratio of aggregate social expenditure to GDP. It also considers, in a sometimes speculative vein, the larger policy issues that are implied. Subsequent chapters examine the economic and demographic assumptions and the methodology of the study, the results of the projections for the major social expenditure programs—pensions, medical care, education, unemployment insurance, and family benefits—and some of the key policy issues in these programs. Inter alia, these include such issues as the effect on pension expenditure of a later retirement age or of linking pensions to net-of-tax rather than gross wages, and the impact on medical care expenditure of efforts to contain medical costs. The sectoral chapters also indicate the types of policy actions that have been introduced by the different countries to stem the likely growth in expenditure.

Principal Results of the Study

The study required demographic projections for each of the seven major industrial countries. In general, the baseline scenario assumes an increase in fertility rates[5] and a modest improvement in life expectancies at birth over their present levels. Such scenarios are in most cases similar to the middle scenarios used by the national authorities. Alternative "greater aging" scenarios are also evaluated in light of the possibility that fertility rates may fail to rise above their current low levels and that medical progress may make it possible to sustain a somewhat longer life expectancy. In effect, the demographic situation implied by current demographic parameters is largely within the range implied by the two alternative scenarios. These projections are discussed in greater depth in Chapter III. In summary, there will be a striking increase in the share of the elderly and a reduced share of the young in the population in all of the countries over the next 40 years. In some countries, such as Canada and the United States, these changes will occur only after the year 2010. In others, they have already occurred and will be accentuated over time, as in the Federal Republic of Germany, Italy, and the United Kingdom. In Japan, these changes will come swiftly.

If it is assumed that governments simply maintain the real 1980 per capita level of social benefits for the different age groups, the increase in the total size and the change in the structure of the population would lead to significantly greater social expenditure by 2025, ranging from a 70 percent increase in Canada to a 361 percent increase in Japan. However, when viewed relative to the growth in GDP that would be implied by projections of the labor force and historically reasonable productivity assumptions, these increased expenditures appear financially manageable. In Canada, France, the United Kingdom, and the United States, the ratio of social expenditure to GDP would actually decrease; in the Federal Republic of Germany, Italy, and Japan, the increases would be moderate, ranging from 1 to 4 percentage points of GDP. In other words, the growth in government social expenditure strictly implied by demographic factors alone can be realistically financed. Unfortunately, to assume that real 1980 benefit levels can be held constant is not realistic.

In particular, in most pension programs real benefits are typically linked to real wage rates, and as the latter increase with productivity so would the former under present policies. Efforts to cut the linkage by significantly lowering the "replacement rate" (i.e., the ratio of a pension to the last period's wage level) would require a change in the implicit pension contract that might be politically difficult to enact. It is equally difficult to expect that real salaries in the medical and education industries would fail to keep pace with the growth in aggregate productivity in the economy. Given the labor intensity of these industries, such wage increases are likely to be translated into an increase in real per capita expenditure. In fact, the experience of the past two decades suggests that it will be difficult simply to contain the growth of real benefit levels in medical care programs to that of productivity.

As a result, the projections of social expenditure in this study require assumptions about the relationship between the growth in real benefit levels and that of productivity in the economy.[6] The specific assumptions underlying the benefit levels in the different programs, as well as the likely obstacles associated with cost containment in education and medical care are discussed in the following chapters. As much as possible, such assumptions attempt to take account of recent policies to contain costs or limit the growth of benefits.

[5] The fertility rate is based on the average number of live births to a woman over her reproductive lifetime. A fertility rate of approximately 2.1 is necessary for a nation, over time and with no net immigration, to reproduce itself. As the results of this study indicate, fertility rates below 2.1 can prevail for a long time before the rate of growth in the population actually turns negative (given the past fertility rates and the existing age structure of the population).

[6] The projections assume an underlying baseline economic scenario, specified principally in terms of the rate of growth of productivity and the assumed unemployment rate. An alternative, more pessimistic economic scenario is also evaluated in conjunction with the "greater aging" demographic scenario. Given that the underlying model assumes a direct link between the growth in real benefit levels and that of productivity, the economic scenario chosen has its principal impact on expenditure on unemployment compensation. See Chapter II for a fuller discussion of these issues.

The implied growth in overall expenditure is thus less than would have been obtained with a simple extrapolation of the growth in real benefit levels experienced over the past two and a half decades. As will be seen, an important implication of this study is that there will be a need for additional policy measures to contain the real increase in per capita benefits, especially in those countries with high tax rates.

The principal conclusions for each of the countries are provided below. In brief, the projections to the year 2025 indicate a significant increase in the ratio of government social expenditure to GDP in most of the countries except Canada, and particularly sharp increases in most of the European countries and Japan (Chart 1 and Table 14). For illustrative purposes, the magnitude of the implied net additional financing burden can be expressed by relating it to the total wage bill in the economy. In effect, suppose the *net increase* in expenditure was to be financed exclusively through the payroll tax. Chart 2 provides a rough estimate of the increase over recent payroll tax rates that would be required to fund the additional burden.[7] The tax rate would have to increase by 7 percentage points in France and by as much as 21 percentage points in Japan. This higher burden would be associated with a substantial increase in intergenerational financial transfers from the working-age population to the elderly.

The timing of the increased pressure for social expenditure by government differs across countries, emerging before the end of this century in the Federal Republic of Germany, Italy, and Japan. In France and the United Kingdom, projections show only a modest increase in the ratio of social expenditure to GDP through the year 2010, with sharper increases between 2010 and 2025. In Canada and the United States, the expenditure ratio will *decrease* until 2010. In both countries, the ratio would then increase in the following 15 years, but in Canada the increase would still be very limited. In terms of specific programs, a steady increase is projected for the ratio of government medical expenditure to GDP in all countries. The timing of the change in the pension expenditure ratio will largely mirror the change in the share of the elderly in the population. The ratio of government education expenditure to GDP will fall in the next 15 years, stabilizing thereafter.

In reviewing the individual country results, one should again caution that countries differ both in their definition of what is included in "government social expenditure" and in the relative importance of the public and private sectors in its provision and financing. In countries where the private sector is relatively

Chart 1. Ratio of Expenditure to GDP for Total Government Social Expenditure, 1980–2025

(In percent)

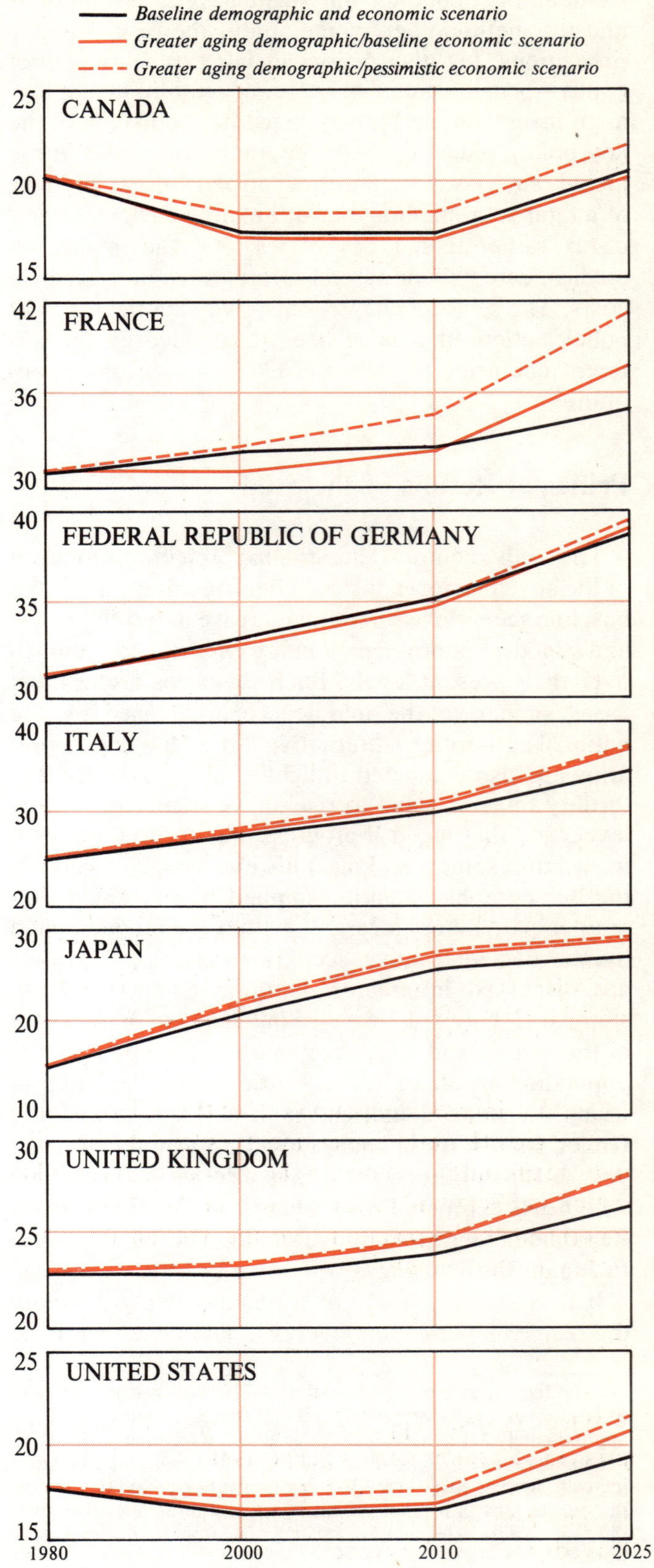

[7] It should be noted that the existing payroll tax presently finances only a portion of government social expenditure.

Chart 2. Implied Change in Payroll Tax Rate Arising from Changes in the Government's Social Expenditure Burden, 1980–2025

(In percent)

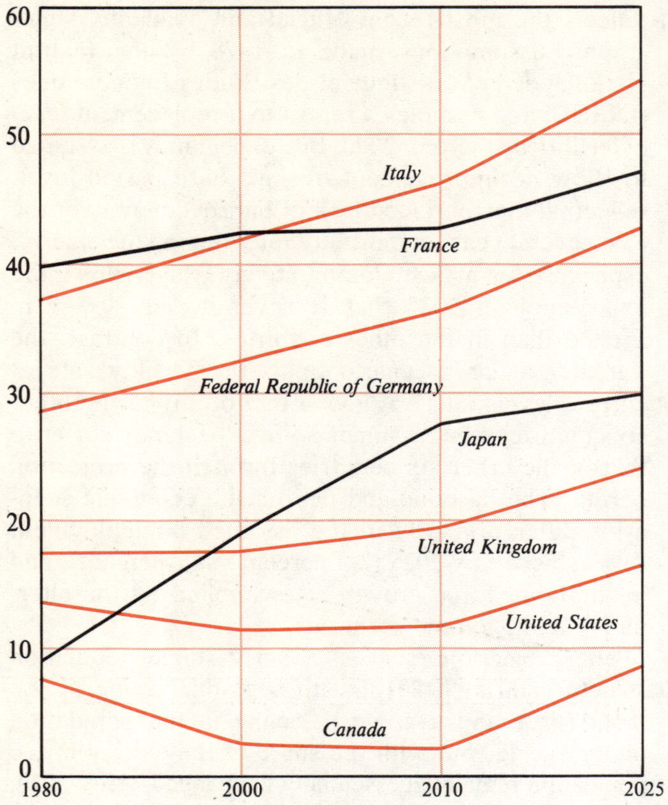

Source: Organization for Economic Cooperation and Development, *The Tax/Benefit Position of Production Workers: 1979–1983* (1984).

[1] This chart assumes that the net change in government social expenditure since 1980 is financed by an increase in the payroll tax relative to the rate levied in 1983. The 1983 tax rate is calculated by dividing the employee and employer's contributions by the income of the average production worker (the latter being augmented by the employer's contribution).

important in providing support for the elderly, focus on the growth in the government's social expenditure will significantly understate the overall resource allocation implications of the growth in the share of the elderly in the population (see the section on Broad Policy Issues below).

Canada

While Canada appears to be subject to the same process of demographic change as the other six major industrial countries, reflecting a historically declining fertility rate and an increasing life expectancy, it is far less advanced in the process. Coupled with a relatively lower level of government social benefits, particularly in the area of pensions, and a correspondingly lower overall ratio of government social expenditure to GDP, the more dramatic effects of the aging process on the expenditure ratio are not likely to occur at least through the year 2025. This is particularly the case under current policy provisions, whereby the flat-rate pension (Old Age Security), family allowance benefits, and the Canada Assistance Plan are indexed to prices and not to earnings (and have been for many years).

In 1980, Canada's government social expenditure ratio was among the lowest of the seven major industrial countries—20 percent of GDP. Equally important, the ratio of pension expenditure to GDP was substantially less than in any of the other six countries, reflecting relatively lower average pension benefits and a low share of the elderly in the population. Though its fertility rate has recently declined to a level comparable with the rates of Japan, the United Kingdom, and the United States, its age structure is much younger, particularly in terms of the share of the population under age 40 (matched only by the United States).

The declining fertility rate will gradually have an impact on the age structure of Canada's population, even with a baseline scenario calling for a return by 2010 to the level of fertility (2.1) required to maintain a constant population size (from approximately 1.9 in 1980). It will be reflected initially in a decline in the share of the under-15 age group in the population by 2000. The structure of the population aged 20–64 will also shift sharply, with the share of the group aged 20–29 declining from 32 percent to 21 percent between 1980 and 2000, and with a significant increase in the share of the group aged 40–49. The significant increase in the share of the elderly and in the elderly dependency rate[8] will principally occur after 2010. Between 2010 and 2025, the share of the elderly in the population will rise from almost 13 percent to almost 19 percent. The population will grow at a rate of over 1 percent annually through the year 2000 but will then markedly decelerate in the first quarter of the century. Assuming that Canada's productivity growth becomes comparable to that in the United States, its real GDP growth will be close to 3 percent through 2000, and then will decline, reflecting the decelerating growth in the labor force.

The baseline scenario projects a decline in the ratio of government social expenditure to GDP in the next 15 years, with a resurgence in the ratio occurring only after the year 2010, and even then leading to only a

[8] The elderly dependency rate is defined as the ratio of the population aged 65 and over to the potential working-age population (aged 15–64). The youth dependency rate is the ratio of the population under age 15 to the same denominator.

modest increase over the 1980 level (equivalent to 0.5 percentage points of GDP) by 2025. The ratios to GDP of expenditure on education, family allowance benefits, and expenses under the Canada Assistance Plan are projected to decline over the whole period, with the education ratio reflecting demographic factors, and the others the continuation of existing policies whereby benefit levels are adjusted only for inflation. Only the ratio of expenditure on medical care to GDP will increase steadily over the period. The ratio of pension expenditure to GDP is expected to decline through 2010, and although it will rise by 40 percent between 2010 and 2025, this increase entails only a one percentage point increase in the ratio to GDP over its 1980 level. In the case of a significant change in benefits policy, this result would no longer hold. In particular, if Old Age Security, family allowance, and Canada Assistance Plan benefits were adjusted in line with earnings rather than prices, the overall ratio of social expenditure to GDP would rise to 24 percent by 2025, rather than almost 21 percent under the baseline scenario. Pension expenditure alone would be 6.6 percent of GDP rather than 4.3 percent. However, the government social expenditure ratio would still decline through 2010 (to 18.5 percent and 19.1 percent of GDP by 2000 and 2010, respectively).

If the fertility rate remained at its current level, there would be a more rapid rate of aging in the population. Coupled with the more pessimistic economic scenario, this would yield an additional increase in the social expenditure ratio of approximately 2 percentage points of GDP by 2025. In both scenarios, these results focus only on government programs; the increase in the overall social expenditure ratio, public and private, would be larger, reflecting the relatively important role of the private sector in the support of the elderly.

France

In 1980, the ratio of government social expenditure to GDP in France was one of the two highest in the seven major industrial countries, equal to that of the Federal Republic of Germany. In demographic terms, the share of the elderly in the population and the elderly dependency rate were both relatively high. The share of the young was comparable to that in the other six countries (though considerably higher than the share in the Federal Republic of Germany). Its fertility rate averaged 1.9 in 1982–83, though it has declined over the past two decades. Even under the relatively optimistic baseline economic scenario and with a demographic scenario showing no increase in life expectancy, the social expenditure ratio to GDP in France will rise through 2025, with the sharpest increase between 2010 and 2025.

There are significant differences between the results of the baseline scenario and those of the "greater aging," more pessimistic economic scenario, particularly in the period 2010–25. The baseline scenario reflects the most recent official and available demographic assumptions made in 1978 by the Institut National de la Statistique et des Etudes Economiques (INSEE) and assumes a return to a replacement level of fertility by the year 2000. Life expectancy is assumed to show no improvement over its base period level, reflecting the continued lack of improvement over the past several years in mortality rates among the elderly, especially for males. Comparatively, this yields a life expectancy in 2025 that is several years lower in France than in the other countries. In contrast, the "greater aging" scenario holds the fertility rate at current levels (at 1.95, above that of any of the other six countries), but assumes a life expectancy closer to that of the other six countries through the projection period. The baseline and pessimistic economic scenarios differ primarily in the assumed unemployment rate achieved by 2025 (2.5 percent vs. 7 percent), and in the labor force growth rates implied by the alternative demographic scenarios.

The projections suggest a fairly stable population structure through 2010, with a gradual aging of the labor force and a modest decline in the population under age 15, but with the share of the elderly in the population remaining essentially unchanged. After 2010, a sharp increase will occur in both the share of the elderly and the elderly dependency rate, with the magnitude of change depending on the rate of improvement in life expectancy. Population growth will be moderate through the year 2000, and then will decelerate strongly thereafter. Real economic growth in the baseline scenario is projected at slightly over 2 percent annually, with the deceleration in the growth of the labor force offset by the decline in the unemployment rate. In the pessimistic economic scenario, real growth falls to less than 2 percent between 2010 and 2025.

Both scenarios suggest a fairly similar picture for the evolution of the government social expenditure ratio through the year 2010. Together, expenditures on pensions and medical care are expected to rise gradually by 3–4 percentage points of GDP. The ratio of education expenditure will decline by 0.5 percent of GDP, principally over the next 15 years. The ratio of unemployment benefits will either rise or fall by approximately 0.5 percent of GDP, depending on the economic scenario. Beyond 2010, the results of the scenarios diverge more sharply. Under the baseline scenario, the social expenditure ratio would rise by an additional 2.5 percent of GDP by 2025; under the "greater aging," more pessimistic economic scenario, it would rise by almost 7 percent of GDP, with these increases primarily arising from higher pension and medical care expenditure.

Finally, much of the rapid growth in the social expenditure ratio in France in the past two decades has stemmed from nondemographic factors. The projection model assumes that these sources of growth will be largely contained, reflecting the almost universal coverage of pension and health programs and recent declines in the relative price effect in the medical care program. If total social expenditure is allowed to rise at the rate experienced in the past decade, the social expenditure ratio would be substantially higher by the year 2000 than in these projections, making the financial pressures accompanying subsequent demographic developments more difficult to cope with.

Federal Republic of Germany

Among the seven major industrial countries, the Federal Republic of Germany had one of the highest ratios of government social expenditure to GDP—31 percent—in 1980. The aging of the population was also the most advanced, with a high share of the elderly in the population (both over 65 and over 75), the smallest share of the young, a high elderly dependency rate, and the lowest youth dependency rate. Its fertility rate of 1.4 was the lowest of the Group of Seven countries—significantly below that required to maintain a constant population size.

The results of the baseline demographic scenario indicate that, even with a significant increase in the fertility rate to almost 1.7, the aging of the population will continue, with the share of the elderly rising steadily to almost a quarter of the population by the year 2025 and the share of the young declining, albeit gradually. The average age of the labor force will sharply increase. The population will *decline* from 62 million in 1980 to 54 million by 2025 (in part reflecting an assumed emigration of 1 million persons by 1990). The labor force will also shrink, on average declining by 0.5 percent annually over the period. Even with a reduction in the unemployment rate over the period, the economic growth rate is likely to be slower than that experienced in the past decade.

The authorities have recently introduced measures to curb the growth in expenditure on pensions and medical care. However, the baseline scenario suggests a continuous increase in the ratio of government social expenditure to GDP, to 33 percent by the end of the century and to 38 percent by 2025. This is primarily due to an expansion in the pension ratio (from 13 percent of GDP in 1980 to almost 21 percent by 2025) but also reflects an increase in the medical expenditure ratio. Some savings will be realized in expenditures on education, unemployment insurance, and other social programs, but only in the next decade or so; no further significant declines in the expenditure ratios for such programs are expected after 1990. These results will be further exacerbated if the fertility rate does not increase and under a more pessimistic economic scenario, with the increased ratio of government social expenditure to GDP emerging between 2010 and 2025. The results clearly imply that if contribution rates are not to rise to excessive levels, a fundamental restructuring of the retirement system will be necessary, most likely implying some combination of lower pension benefits or a later retirement age.

Italy

Like the other European countries, Italy had a high ratio of government social expenditure to GDP in 1980—reaching 25 percent, with much of this devoted to pensions and medical care. The share of the elderly in the population was 13.5 percent in 1980, one fifth of the potential working-age population. As in the Federal Republic of Germany, the fertility rate (1.6) was quite low.

The baseline demographic scenario suggests that, even with an increase in the fertility rate to 1.9 by 2000, the aging of Italy's population will continue, with the share of the elderly in the population rising to almost 16 percent by 2000 and almost 20 percent by 2025, more than one quarter of the potential working-age population. At the same time, the share of the young in the population will decline. The share of the higher-savings group aged 40–60 in the population aged 20–64 will initially decline; however, after 2000, the share of this group will rise at the expense of the group under age 40. Italy's population will peak at 58 million around the year 2000, declining slowly thereafter. These demographic trends will be reflected in a slow growth in the labor force, averaging only 0.1 percent annually. Productivity growth is assumed to increase to 2.2 percent annually, similar to Italy's European neighbors, implying real economic growth of over 2 percent annually (compared with 1.8 percent between 1974 and 1984).

The baseline scenario projects a steady increase in the ratio of government social expenditure to GDP over the period, rising to almost 28 percent in 2000, 30 percent in 2010, and almost 35 percent in 2025. The ratio of pension expenditure to GDP will alone rise from 12 percent in 1980 to almost 21 percent in 2025. The ratio of education expenditure to GDP will decline, but only through 2000. As in the Federal Republic of Germany, a "greater aging," more pessimistic economic scenario will show the greatest impact after 2010, with the ratio of government social expenditure to GDP being higher by 1 percentage point by 2010 and 2.5 percentage points by 2025.

Italy is unique among the Group of Seven in that its social expenditure program is not fully on a pay-as-you-go basis and has already required debt financing. Future working generations are likely to be forced to bear not only the burden of a larger retired population, but also the debt-service burden arising from present deficits. Beyond the obvious measure of an increase in the eligibility age for pensions, most other proposals for change involve more fundamental changes in the social security and welfare systems and measures for cost containment in medical care programs.

Japan

The impact of demographic change on the Japanese economy is likely to be the most extreme among the Group of Seven, reflecting both the lateness with which Japan began the demographic transition to a lower fertility rate and a higher life expectancy, and the sharpness of the change that has been experienced (particularly the decline in fertility in the early 1950s). In 1980, Japan had the lowest ratio of government social expenditure of the seven major industrial countries—15.4 percent of GDP (less than half that of the Federal Republic of Germany), reflecting low ratios of expenditure on pensions and medical care. Japan also appeared the least aged, with the lowest elderly dependency rate (13 percent), the lowest share of the elderly in the population (9 percent), and the highest share of the young. Its fertility rate (1.7) was comparable to that of Canada, the United Kingdom, and the United States.

In the next 40 years, Japan will make the transition to a population structure closely approximating that of the European countries. Compared with other countries, what is striking is the rapidity and magnitude of the change, rather than the ratios of expenditure or the actual population structure that will emerge. Specifically, the elderly dependency rate will rise by 65 percent in the next 15 years (from 13 percent in 1980 to 22 percent by 2000) and will be two and a half times its 1980 level by 2025. In contrast, the youth dependency rate will fall from 35 percent in 1980 to 26 percent in 2000. The share of the elderly will rise from 9 percent of the population in 1980 to 15 percent in 2000 and 21 percent in 2025. With an increasing life expectancy, those aged 75 and over will constitute over half of the elderly population by 2025.

The structure of the population aged 20–64 will also change, with a decline in the share of the under-40 age group from 52 percent in 1980 to 45 percent by 2000. The population will grow rapidly through 2000 but then growth will sharply decelerate. The labor force will grow through 2000 but will then decline thereafter. The baseline economic scenario assumes that Japan will maintain its historically high rate of productivity growth of 3 percent. As a result, the real growth rate is projected at almost 4 percent through 2000, falling to under 3 percent thereafter.

Government social expenditure is projected to rise to 27 percent of GDP by 2025—still considerably less than that of most of the European countries in the Group of Seven. However, the rate of change would be considerably greater, with the social expenditure ratio rising by almost 40 percent through 2000 and by 76 percent through 2025. This would imply the need for considerable fiscal adjustment. Pension expenditures will still grow substantially, with the pension expenditure ratio expected to more than double by 2000 and triple by 2025. These increases in pension expenditure are, however, lower than they would have been in the absence of the 1985 Pension Reform Act. Savings in education expenditure are likely to be realized, but by less than 1 percent of GDP. In the event that fertility rates do not rise to replacement levels and under a more pessimistic economic scenario, the social expenditure ratio would be 1 to 2 percentage points of GDP greater throughout the period than in the baseline scenario.

United Kingdom

Government social expenditure in the United Kingdom was approximately 23 percent of GDP in 1980, significantly lower than in some of the other European countries, in part reflecting the relative importance of private pensions. Yet by 1980, the aging of the population had proceeded further in the United Kingdom than in any of the other major industrial countries except the Federal Republic of Germany. The elderly dependency rate of 23 percent was the highest of the Group of Seven, the share of the over-65 age group in the population was approximately 15 percent, and the share of the young was among the lowest. However, in contrast to the Federal Republic of Germany, the fertility rate of 1.8 was well within the range of most of the other major industrial countries, although still lower than that required to ensure a stable population size.

Only modest further aging of the United Kingdom's population is likely to occur through the year 2010, as reflected by a shift in the relative shares of the young and those over age 65. The share of the very old (i.e., over 75) will rise more rapidly. Thereafter, the aging of the population is projected to accelerate, as the share of the elderly will rise from 16 percent of the population by 2010 to almost 19 percent by 2025, primarily at the expense of the share of the working-age population. The elderly dependency rate will rise from 24 percent to 29 percent over the same period. These developments will occur even with an assumed increase in the fertility rate to replacement levels by the year 2010. Given the existing population structure, only limited growth in the labor force can be expected for most of the period (averaging 0.1 percent annually) and real GDP is projected to grow by 1.5 percent annually, compared with the 1.1 percent annual rate in the period 1974–84.

Through the end of the century, virtually no change in the government social expenditure ratio is expected to occur, remaining at 23 percent of GDP. The ratio is then projected to rise to 24 percent by 2010 and to 26.5 percent by 2025. As in the Federal Republic of Germany and Italy, the expenditure ratio on education will decline through the year 2000 and then stabilize thereafter. The ratios of expenditure on medical care and pensions to GDP are projected to rise continuously through the period. The increases in pension expenditure are, however, considerably less than would have emerged in the absence of the reforms proposed in the December 1985 White Paper. If fertility rates remain unchanged, the effects would be principally felt between 2010 and 2025, with the social expenditure ratio rising by an additional percentage point of GDP by 2025 relative to the baseline scenario.

United States

The combination of a comparatively young population, by Group of Seven standards, and a relatively limited involvement by the government in the provision of medical and pension benefits is likely to limit the impact of demographic trends on the growth of government social expenditure in the United States. In fact, the ratio of government social expenditure to GDP—18 percent in 1980—is projected to decline through the year 2010. As in Canada, the aging of the population is likely to be relatively sharp thereafter, resulting in a steady increase in the social expenditure ratio. The impact on the overall allocation of resources will be considerably greater, reflecting the private sector's provision of more than half of total medical expenditure and a quarter of total pension disbursements. Moreover, the shift in the distribution of expenditure among education, health, and pensions is likely to necessitate major structural changes in the distribution of the financing burden at the federal, state, and local levels of government.

In 1980, a relatively high share of the population was under age 40, with a particularly large group between ages 20 and 29. A high immigration rate supplemented a fertility rate that was relatively high (though below the replacement rate) in providing a buoyancy to the population growth rate. Under the baseline demographic scenario, the population should experience a relatively slow process of aging through 2010, with a gradual decline in the share of the young and an increase in the share of the age group 65 and over. There will also be increased aging of the labor force. Within the population aged 20–64, the share of those aged 20–29 will fall from 32 percent to 22 percent. After 2010, the process of retirement of the "baby boom" generation will be reflected by a more than 50 percent increase in the elderly dependency rate; the increase in the share of the elderly in the population will be matched by a decline in the share of the working-age population. The total population is projected to grow by over a third through 2025, reflecting the return to a replacement rate of fertility and continued immigration. The baseline scenario assumes that productivity will be sustained at 1.6 percent annually over the period, implying a deceleration in the growth of real GDP, reflecting the diminishing growth of the labor force.

The overall government social expenditure ratio is expected to decline slightly before the year 2010, reflecting an almost 20 percent drop in the ratio of education expenditure to GDP, a corresponding increase in that for medical care, and a decline in the pension expenditure ratio. Between 2010 and 2025, the social expenditure ratio is projected to rise by almost 20 percent, or 3 percent of GDP. However, the growth in the overall resources required to support the elderly should be significantly greater, given the private sector's role in providing for the needs of the elderly.

Since the bulk of government medical expenditure is focused on the elderly, the sharp aging of the population after 2010 will imply a significant increase in the share of medical care expenditure financed by the government. Education expenditure is expected to fall from almost 30 percent of total government social expenditure to less than 20 percent, suggesting the need to shift some of the burden of revenue absorption from the local to the federal level of government or to shift expenditure responsibilities. Finally, it should be noted that these projections reflect recent measures to limit the future growth of pension expenditure, following the adoption of some of the recommendations of the National Commission on Social Security Reform, known as the Greenspan Commission (1983). This underscores the sensitivity of the results to projections of medical care expenditure, with the ratio of nonmedical social expenditure declining relative to GDP.

Robustness of Projections to Assumptions

For most of the countries in this study, the projections suggest that the prospective growth in social expenditure is likely to be daunting, even in those cases where this growth will not occur for many years. How robust are these estimates? To what assumptions do they prove particularly sensitive? What problems have been excluded from the analysis which could affect the dynamics of the growth in social expenditure? What are the key policy issues that will need to be addressed during the period? This section addresses these questions.

Demographic Assumptions

The study has attempted to delimit a range of alternative patterns of fertility and mortality through its use of two demographic scenarios: one that closely approximates the most recent official projections, the other embodying demographic assumptions implying "greater aging." In most cases, the baseline assumptions should be regarded as being reasonable, if not optimistic (in terms of "slower aging"), to the extent that they project a significant increase in fertility rates to replacement levels. A continuation of fertility rates at their present low levels is embodied in the "greater aging" scenario. The projections of expenditure in the latter scenario generally suggest only a moderate accentuation of the patterns derived from the baseline assumptions.

The individual country assumptions also implicitly assume that significant differences in unemployment rates can persist among the European countries over a 45-year period but this should not markedly affect the results (see Chapter II). Alternative immigration scenarios have also not been modeled systematically. The range of immigration assumptions across countries is fairly wide. In the Federal Republic of Germany, it is assumed that a net emigration of a million persons, principally returning migrant workers, will occur over the period 1980–90, with no further movement thereafter—a net *emigration* rate of 1.6 individuals per thousand; in Canada and the United States, a net *immigration* rate of 1.6 and 4.2 individuals, respectively, per thousand is assumed. Immigration rules are an important, but controversial, policy instrument available to national decision makers that could affect the underlying demographic and economic parameters and have important sociological and economic consequences.

A change in national policies toward immigration, particularly in some of the European countries and possibly Japan, would obviously qualify these projections. It could change both the size and composition of the labor pool, the age composition of the population (and the associated dependency rates), overall fertility rates, the level and structure of demand for different social services, and the wage base for financing social expenditure programs and transfers.

Time Frame of the Study

The projections of this study focus on the period 1980–2025. Does limiting the time frame to 2025 significantly bias the results, by omitting any marked structural changes that occur in the years thereafter? This question is particularly relevant for Canada and the United States—the two countries where the effects of aging appear to emerge only after the year 2010. For the United States, the years 2025–40 are likely to see a further aging of the population, though the pace of aging, as measured by the increase in the elderly dependency rate, will decelerate.[9] The composition of the elderly population is projected to shift markedly, however. Between 1980 and 2025, the share of the group aged 75 and over among the elderly is expected to rise from 40 percent to 43 percent; in the next 15 years, it should increase to 56 percent. While such a change will not have dramatic effects on pension expenditure, it does have implications for medical expenditure, as the very elderly have higher medical expenditure per capita. Fund staff estimates suggest that, under the baseline demographic scenario, the social expenditure ratio will rise by an additional percentage point of GDP and, under the "greater aging" scenario, by approximately 2½ percentage points, between 2025 and 2040. In Canada, the projections suggest a further increase in the share of the elderly and in the elderly dependency rate, which is likely to be reflected in a higher social expenditure ratio by 2035.[10]

Economic Assumptions

A number of important uncertainties are associated with the effects of an aging population on the structure and size of the labor force and on the rate of growth

[9] In the baseline scenario, the elderly dependency rate rises from 35 percent by 2025 to 38 percent by 2030 and 40 percent by 2040. In the "greater aging" scenario, it rises from 41 percent by 2025 to 52 percent by 2040.

[10] The share of the elderly is projected to peak at almost 22 percent by 2035, compared with over 19 percent by 2025, with the elderly dependency rate rising to 36 percent, compared with 31 percent by 2025.

of productivity. Population aging will be accompanied by a slowdown in the growth rate of the working-age population; in the Federal Republic of Germany, the growth rate will actually decline. In some cases, this is assumed to lead to increased labor force participation and lower unemployment rates. At the same time, the labor force will progressively age (see Chapter III). In some countries over the next two decades, a marked shift will be seen in the relative shares of the labor force in the 20–29 age bracket vis-à-vis the 40–49 age group (e.g., Canada, United States) or vis-à-vis the 50–59 age group (e.g., Japan). In Japan, a sharp decline in the size of the age group 30–50 will be seen—from 52 percent of the population aged 20–64 to 43 percent. In other countries, such as the Federal Republic of Germany, the next 15 years will see a sharp decline in the share of the 20–29 age group in the labor force, compared with the share of those over age 50.

A simple life-cycle model could be constructed whereby such changes would influence the rate of technological progress and the rate of productivity growth in the economy, but the direction of causality would be ambiguous. Do the more fundamental innovations in basic knowledge derive from a large and vibrant younger segment of the population? Some argue that an individual's productivity peaks between the ages of 30 and 45. There is empirical evidence that suggests that productivity increases with aging in the labor force, though the range of historical experience may not capture the changes in aging that are likely to occur in these countries (Wachter (1976), p. 127). On that basis, the sharp increase in the share of the labor force in these groups in Canada and the United States should bolster productivity in the next two decades. On the other hand, there may be limits as to how rapidly the rate of technological progress or the rate of productivity growth among the key industrial countries can diverge, particularly over a 45-year time frame.

Other life-cycle factors will have an impact on the prospective growth of productivity. Of the working-age population, the highest-savings groups are those between ages 40 and 60. In Canada and the United States, the share of these groups in the population aged 20–64 is expected to rise by 10 to 14 percentage points, compared with only 2–4 percentage point increases in France, Japan, and the United Kingdom, and declining shares in the Federal Republic of Germany and Italy. Does this suggest the likelihood of a change in savings and investment rates? As an added uncertainty, will perceptions of an aging population and doubts about the adequacy of government social insurance benefits induce a higher savings rate in the economy? Savings rates might increase, simply reflecting an individual's awareness that life expectancy is increasing and that the amount of private retirement savings necessary to complement public pension benefits may need to be augmented.

In terms of the projections of the study, the key issue is whether changes in the growth of productivity will influence the growth in real benefits or per capita expenditure for the principal beneficiary groups. In the case of education and medical care, the projections tend to assume either that such expenditures rise at the same rate as productivity (as with education) or by a constant factor in excess of productivity (as with medical care), primarily reflecting the labor intensity of the production function of these services and the assumption that the specialized factors of production in these sectors maintain their relative income position. As a result, the projections for these programs are *not* particularly sensitive to the productivity assumptions. The driving force behind the growth in the ratios of medical and education expenditures to GDP is, in most cases, the difference between the growth in the number of beneficiaries and that of the active labor force.[11]

In the case of pensions, the relationship is a bit more complex. Certainly, it would be expected that the *starting* pension of any retiring person would be linked to the wage or salary level received in the years prior to retirement and thus would be affected by productivity trends. In the 1960s and 1970s, there was also a tendency to link the pension benefits of *already retired* individuals to the growth in real wages in the economy—in effect, correcting not only for the effects of inflation (e.g., at least maintaining the pensioner's standard of living in real terms) but also adjusting it to maintain the pensioner's relative income position as well. In recent years, there has been a withdrawal from the expectation that the latter adjustment would necessarily occur, so that a higher rate of productivity in principle, with no inflation, would not necessarily be associated with an adjustment of the pensions of those already past retirement age.[12] This situation would imply that higher productivity growth would reduce the ratio of pension expenditure to GDP. On the other hand, if the economic climate changed and productivity rose substantially above current rates,

[11] This statement is subject to the qualification that the growth of employment is not fully independent of productivity growth. In the projections, different productivity trends are associated with different long-term unemployment rates that change the size of the active labor force to some extent. But the influence on expenditure as a share of GDP turns out to be minimal.

[12] There is the associated issue of whether pension benefits should be adjusted in line with consumer prices. It has been argued that it would be more reasonable to adjust pension benefits in line with real net wages (e.g., in situations where pensioners should not be any more insulated from inflation than other strata of the labor force). Similarly, to the extent that net real wages decline as a result of the need to increase tax rates, should pension benefits be adjusted in line with gross wages, again improving the relative income position of pensioners?

the pressures on policymakers to adjust pensions could be particularly strong.

There are situations in which the factors determining the growth of productivity in the key productive sectors of the economy, and thus wage rates, may differ from the factors driving total GDP per employee. For example, suppose a nation perceived correctly that it would be necessary to increase its national savings rate and build up its stock of real capital in anticipation of the need to draw down on this capital in order to finance future social expenditure. This could lead to a higher capital-labor ratio but also to increased foreign lending and equity participations abroad, with the return on such capital being reinvested. The growth in income derived from foreign investment and lending would not necessarily be reflected in increased productivity in the domestic economy, nor in increased wage rates or costs in the various social service programs. In this sense, there would be a less direct linkage between the growth in total income per capita and productivity as a factor influencing wage rates. This might be a difficult policy for the group of industrial countries to pursue simultaneously, but in the national interest of individual countries, it might be a rational approach.

Sectoral Assumptions

Subsequent chapters (Chapters IV though VII) discuss some of the specific policy measures that might be introduced to modify the linkage between the growth in productivity and that of real benefits or expenditure per recipient. For example, the "replacement rate" (i.e., the formula relating initial pension benefits to previous earnings levels) can be lowered and the initial age of receipt of a full pension can be raised. To control the growth of expenditure for medical care, limits can be placed on government spending, as in the case of the United Kingdom, the copayment rates of individuals can be raised, and individual medical voucher plans can be introduced in connection with prepaid health plans.

It is important to emphasize that such a weakening of the link between the growth in costs or benefits per recipient and productivity can have a fairly dramatic effect in terms of moderating the growth in social expenditure. Over a 45-year period, benefits per capita rising at an annual rate 0.5 percentage points less than assumed could reduce absolute expenditure by approximately 20 percent. That could virtually eliminate any increase in the social expenditure ratio for all countries in the Group of Seven except Italy and Japan, and it would imply a significant decline from the present ratio in Canada, France, and the United States. Although it would be difficult to achieve such a reduction in real benefit levels, it is still important to underscore the sensitivity of the projections to these assumptions.

In fact, it should be stressed that there are other offsetting pressures that will complicate the task of limiting the growth of costs within the bounds assumed in this study. This is particularly the case for medical insurance programs but also, over the medium term, for education as well. In the former, new technologies may lead to a rapid buildup in medical costs. Recently developed procedures to clean out arteries, to disintegrate kidney stones, or to transplant organs are likely to tap a strong, latent demand for new and expensive forms of medical care. In some cases, such technologies may reduce the overall cost of treatment for an illness, but this may be offset by the increased demand for care they may induce. The pressures for an expansion of medical expenditure even in an efficiently organized medical care system, will be great; withstanding these pressures will inevitably require difficult decisions, involving equity and ethics, as to who will receive financing for many of the expensive procedures or whether such procedures should be rationed.

In the education sector, the next 15 years will most likely see a sharp contraction in the demand for educational services, in view of the anticipated decline in the number of students. The projection model in this study effectively assumes the maintenance of constant teacher-pupil ratios in the face of such a contraction in almost all of the countries. Tenure rules in public education systems may be a significant obstacle to reducing the number of teachers employed.

Broad Policy Issues

Structural Financial Adjustments Related to Shifts in Demand

Adjustments are likely to be necessary in real factor and product markets associated with the shift in the structure of demand for social and other services (for example, out of education and other child-oriented services and products and into medical care and other products and services catering to the elderly). These changes are likely to be more significant than would be indicated in the projections. Even in countries where the government's role is predominant in the provision of social services, there still remains an asymmetry between the young and the aged segments of the population in terms of their relative dependence on government intervention for their overall support. The only element of youth care involving substantial government expenditures appears to be education. A comprehensive accounting for the shifts in absorption of economic resources implied by the prospective demographic changes would have to trace also the relative decline in private expenditures for food, shelter, clothing, entertainment, and in some countries, medical care. This was beyond the scope of this study.

In the next 15 years, a need will also arise to develop alternative arrangements for the financing of social programs. Some countries, notably France, the Federal Republic of Germany, Italy, and Japan, will experience pressures either to increase tax and contribution rates or to reduce benefits in order to meet the increased burden implied by the potential growth of social expenditure. In some countries, increased tax burdens might be feasible, or politically acceptable, only if associated with reforms yielding a more equitable distribution of the burden.

Financing of social programs may require alternative or additional institutional arrangements. Such financing might involve the establishment of private schemes complementary to the existing state pension system, thus allowing for an increasing role of voluntary contributions in countries where private pensions play a limited role. Existing institutional arrangements that imply the emergence of surpluses in one fiscal account and growing deficits in others will also need to be reconciled. This is particularly the case with respect to the withdrawal of resources from education, which is largely the prerogative of state and local governments, and the addition of resources to pension and medical insurance programs, for which the expenditures tend to be managed at the central government level. It also applies in instances where cross-financing presently occurs between various retirement schemes (for example, those of wage earners vs. self-employed) and where the financial viability of cross-financing will become increasingly difficult.

In principle, in the European countries and Japan, shifting resources from the local level to the central government should not be difficult (though such a shift runs counter to recent trends, which have shown an increased role for the local authorities in some countries). Most resource mobilization occurs at the central government level, with the local governments receiving either transfers or designated shares of particular taxes. Inevitably, the intersectoral shift of resources will necessitate a renegotiation of these earmarking formulas, with obvious political ramifications. In Canada and the United States, the state or provincial and local governments are not only responsible for education expenditure but they also finance such expenditure principally from local taxes. In both countries, the need for a substantial increase in expenditure on pensions and medical care at the central government level will not occur until after 2010, so that social expenditure considerations will not be the factor dictating any obvious realignment of revenue bases between the central and local government accounts until that time.

An interesting issue that will arise in these two countries is the response of local governments to the decline in expenditure required in the education sector. Will there be a commensurate reduction in state and local government taxes, or will there be a ratchet effect, as increased funding of other goods and services is provided, with no diminution in local government tax rates? It can be imagined that increasing pressures by the central government will force the local governments either to pick up a larger share of the burden of financing of other social expenditures (for example, by requiring a higher share of financing of Medicaid outlays by the states in the United States) or to lower tax rates. In the United States, both the recent elimination of revenue sharing and the threat of elimination of deductibility from income tax of state and local government taxes may possibly be seen as a reaction to the need for restructuring of fiscal responsibilities.

New Demands and the Public-Private Mix

This study attempts to gauge the impact of demographic trends and other factors on expenditure for existing social expenditure programs. Less predictable, but no less certain, is that new candidates for government expenditure in the social sphere are likely to emerge. The most obvious will relate to the needs of the very elderly (i.e., those over age 80). This group will never be a large share of the population, but its absolute size will triple or quadruple in many countries over the period. As will be discussed in Chapter V, over and above the medical needs of this group, there will be a need for a dramatic expansion in long-term care facilities as well—a need that is largely *not* covered in most existing government social service programs.[13]

This need also highlights the important role of the private sector in the financing of social expenditure in some countries. In the United States, a significant component of medical and educational services, as well as the consumption by the elderly, is effectively financed from private sector resources. The projections in this study for the United States are likely to be reasonably comprehensive with respect to the acute medical needs of the elderly population (and some chronic care), given the coverage of Medicare and Medicaid, but private sector wealth and pensions

[13] See United States, U.S. Congress, Senate (1984); and Kinnaird, Brotherston, and Williamson (1981).

account for a sizable share of the financing of the needs of the elderly. As a result, the increase in the share of total output that will need to be allocated to finance the remaining consumption needs of the elderly (including some chronic medical care) is likely to be considerably greater than that reflected in the projections of government expenditure on pensions. While private sector pensions are less important in the European countries, Canada, and Japan, the role of household savings and intergenerational transfers is still important in some cases. For example, in Japan, public pensions appear at present to be only a basic form of support for most elderly Japanese, with heavy reliance placed on wage income, other sources of income (presumably capital income), and support by their families (in fact, about two thirds of the group aged 65 and over live with their children). While receipts from government pensions are likely to become more significant as such pension programs mature, there will still be a need for additional private sector resources.

However, without understating the important potential role of private sector resources in supporting the elderly, it must be emphasized that the increasing share of the elderly in the population is likely to pose overall macroeconomic problems in financing the associated intergenerational transfer of resources, and these problems transcend the issue of the division of responsibility between the public and private sectors. Simply transferring increased responsibility to the private sector will not significantly diminish the share of resources in the economy that will be needed to support the elderly population, though it may lead to revised incentives in the present working population relating to savings and consumption.

Implications for Macroeconomic Surveillance

An important question that emerges from this study is whether reasonably predictable long-term structural financial problems in the major industrial nations (be they the growth in social expenditure or the implications of rising public debt-service obligations), with possible ramifications for the balance of payments, should either prompt current policy action by the authorities or imply serious constraints on the range of macroeconomic policy options presently available to them. The results of this study suggest that important policy problems confront some of the Group of Seven countries. For Italy and Japan, the problem is more urgent, either because of the rapidity of the likely change, as in the case of Japan, or when viewed in terms of an inability to finance even existing social insurance programs on a pay-as-you-go basis, as in the case of Italy. For others, such as France and the Federal Republic of Germany, a growing pressure on public expenditure may appear manageable in an aggregate financing sense, but will necessitate difficult policy measures in the areas of pensions and medical care and limit the sphere of action for other policies. In particular, actions to provide additional fiscal stimulus to these economies must contend with the fact that such a stimulus may increase the likely ratio of public sector interest expenditure to GDP at a time in the future when tax rates and social benefit regimes are likely to be subject to increased demand pressures. Consideration of the implications of such problems may also affect one's views on the appropriateness of a country's current macroeconomic and balance of payments stance.

The fiscal problems arising from social expenditure trends in the major industrial countries are likely to become far more serious after 2010, notwithstanding the great uncertainties surrounding projections so far into the future. While such problems may pose less urgent constraints on today's policies, failure to take present action will most likely result in more serious policy dilemmas in the future. The problem of financing social expenditure demands in the first half of the next century is likely to engender important intergenerational conflict at that time. Clearly, there are policy actions that countries could be considering now, in anticipation, that would lessen the severity of this problem. Among these, the effectiveness of policies to raise national savings and investment rates should be explored.

There is clearly a question as to the adequacy of the current savings rate in those countries where the problem will become more serious after the year 2010 (see King (1983)). At present, are social insurance schemes effectively viewed by much of the present working population as substitutable for savings? Will the present rate of capital accumulation be sufficient to generate additional income to supplement government pension receipts when the financial pressures on government insurance schemes become intense? Policies to encourage higher savings by the current working-age generation will necessarily clarify and confirm the fact that this generation is likely to have to fund both its own and its parents' retirement.[14] The notion would be the actuarial one of ensuring that a sufficient capital stock is developed to finance some of the burden of supporting the elderly population, thus facilitating a lower overall tax burden on the wage incomes of the working population of that time. An

[14] This could also affect tax reform efforts: for instance, the numerous proposals for expenditure taxes that favor current savings but tax the expenditure from accumulated savings.

equally interesting question is how to ensure an adequate rate of return from a higher national savings rate, particularly if a number of industrial countries attempt to increase their overall investment rates. Will this lead to an increase in investments in Third World countries? What are the issues associated with the ultimate repatriation of this capital? This gives rise to many other systemic questions on the evolving structure of world capital markets and trade flows.

Other current policy actions may be needed either to dampen the likely long-term financial impact of current trends (e.g., policies to contain medical costs) or to begin the process of adjustment to the fundamental structural changes in the economy that will parallel the aging of the labor force. The possibility of encouraging increased immigration may need to be carefully examined in light of the demographic pressures of an aging population.

II Methodology for Projections

Pattern of Government Social Expenditure, 1980

An important problem faced in undertaking this study, particularly given its cross-country focus, was how to define the social expenditure of the government. Clearly, one should include expenditure on education, medical care, pensions, unemployment compensation, and income maintenance for the poor. The dividing line then becomes blurred. Should one include expenditure on family allowances? veterans benefits? workmen's compensation? Should pensions of central government or public enterprise employees be included or treated analogously to the pension expenditure associated with private sector employees? Unfortunately, any cross-country comparison of government social expenditure by program is fraught with methodological difficulties, particularly for the governments of the seven major industrial countries. The structure of programs, the degree of public sector involvement, the instruments of intervention, and the level of benefits vary widely—thus rendering any comparison subject to numerous caveats.

In the individual country studies, the typical definition of social expenditure by government was that used by the country itself, though with the constraint that certain categories of government expenditure were to be included (e.g., medical care, education, welfare payments, pension expenditure, and unemployment insurance). Expenditures at both the general and local government levels were generally included. Pension expenditure was included if the government intermediated its financing—admittedly yielding some incomparabilities across countries in that the pension schemes of some public enterprises might be included in one country and not in another. Similarly, as countries differ in the extent to which the private sector participates in the financing of education and medical expenditure, differences will arise in the magnitude of government social expenditure across countries. Direct housing expenditures were omitted, given the difficulties of fully capturing the off-budget credit and tax subsidies accorded to the housing sector in some countries. Tax expenditures were excluded. These differences do not vitiate the analysis, but rather emphasize the relative importance of examining the movements *across time* in the level of a country's social expenditure in response to demographic or other factors, rather than the differences *across countries* in expenditure ratios at a given point in time.

With these cautions in mind, the variation in the magnitude of the government social expenditure ratio is striking. It ranges from about 15–18 percent in Japan and the United States to as high as 31 percent in France and the Federal Republic of Germany (Chart 3 and Table 15). Much of this variability stems from the difference in the pension expenditure ratio, ranging from less than about 4 percent of GDP in Canada and Japan to over 13 percent in the Federal Republic of Germany (though some of this variability is spurious, reflecting classification difficulties between pension and other expenditures).

The differences in ratios may also be misleading to the extent that they do not take account of tax expenditure and private sector social expenditure. It is useful to indicate the relative importance of these factors. Only limited data are available on tax expenditure[15] and for only five of the countries concerned (Canada, France, the Federal Republic of Germany, the United Kingdom, and the United States). In three of the five countries (France, the United Kingdom, and the United States), inclusion of tax expenditure on social purposes adds significantly to social expenditure (by approximately 1–2 percent of GDP). Inclusion of private sector expenditure on medical care and education and private pension plan disbursements greatly reduces the variability between most of the seven major industrial countries, but significant differences still remain (Chart 3 and Table 16). For example, in 1980 Japan's social expenditure ratio was still approximately half that of France and the Federal Republic of Germany. Inclusion of private sector expenditure suggests that only in the case of the United States and perhaps Canada, does a focus on government expenditure give a misleading picture

[15] These derive principally from unpublished work of the Organization for Economic Cooperation and Development (OECD).

Corrigendum

Aging and Social Expenditure in the Major Industrial Countries, 1980–2025

In Chart 3, page 17, the order of countries depicted by the bars should read as follows:

Canada, France, Fed. Rep. of Germany, Italy, Japan, United Kingdom, United States.

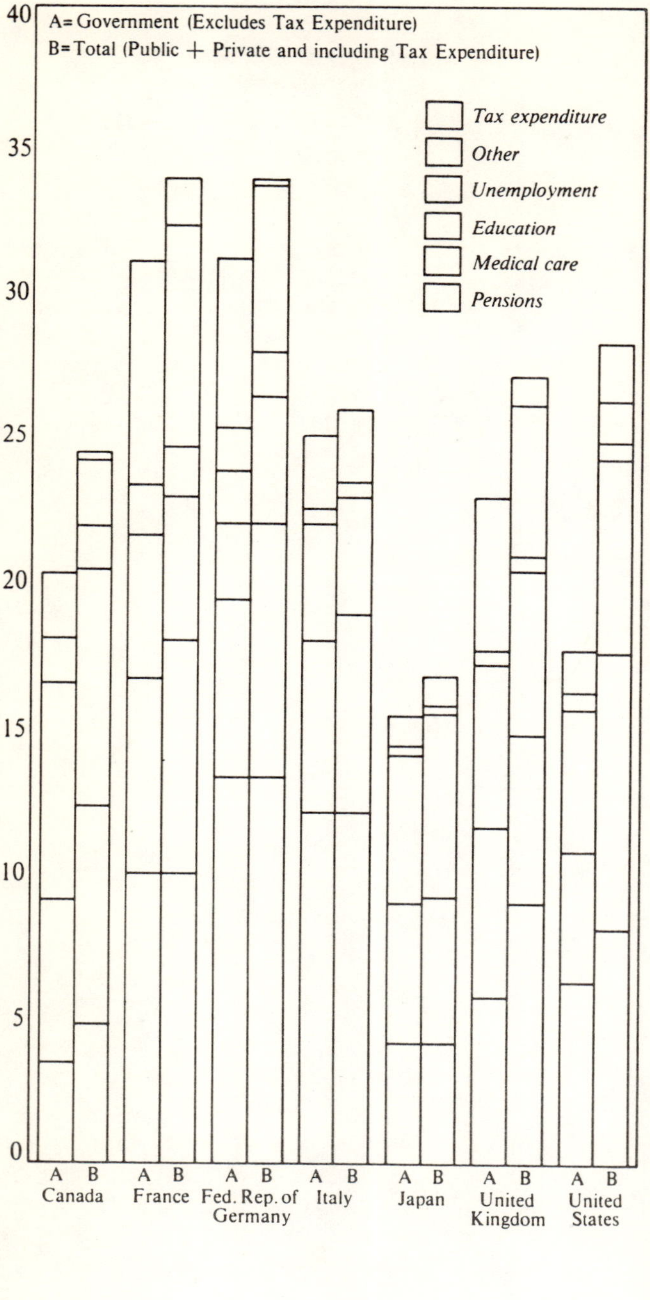

Chart 3. Social Expenditure as a Percentage of GDP by Sector, 1980

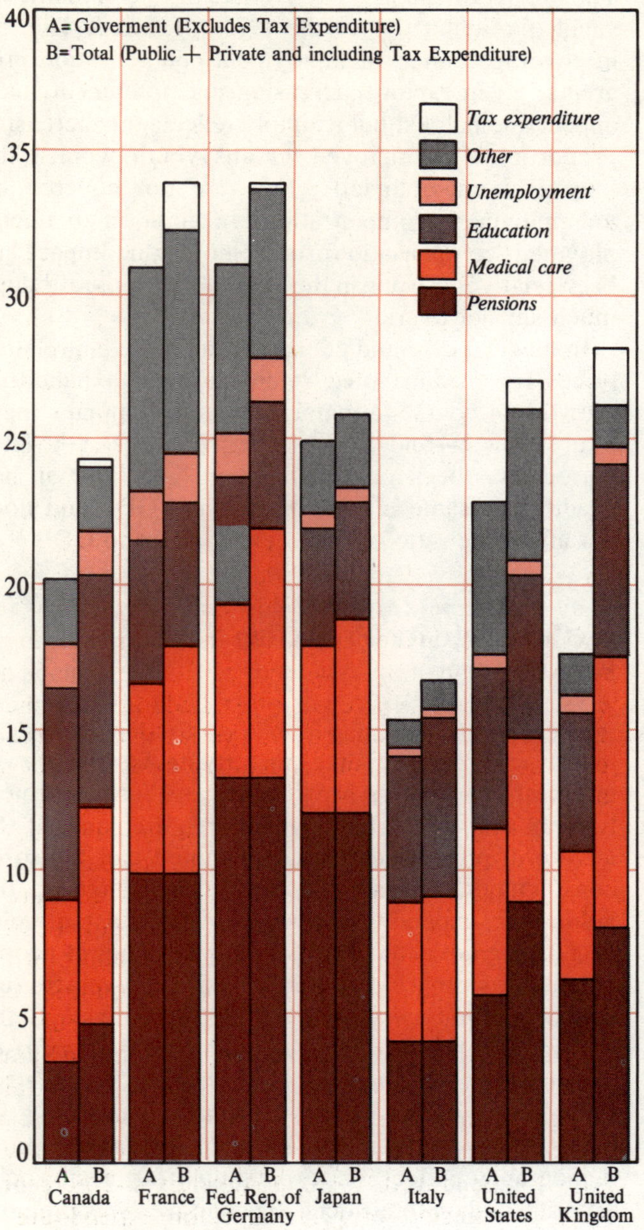

Source: Tables 15 and 16.

Chart 4. Government Social Expenditure, 1960–81

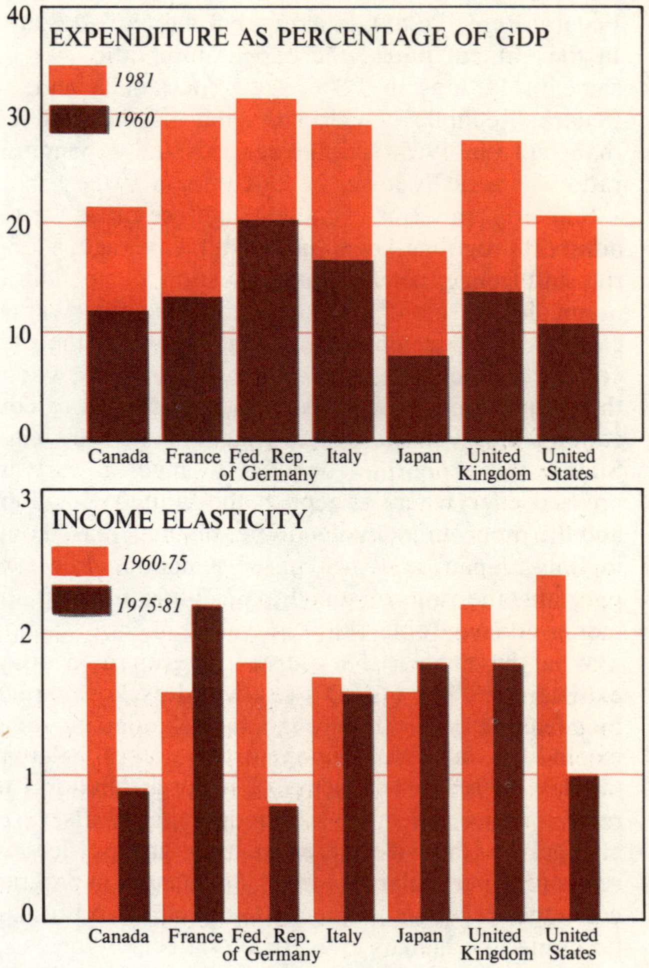

of the magnitude of the social expenditure ratio for the society as a whole. In the case of the United States, almost a third of total social expenditure occurs at the private sector level; in Canada, a quarter.

Much of the growth in social expenditure ratios has occurred since 1960. In a recent OECD study, it is reported that between 1960 and 1981 social expenditure by the governments of the seven major industrial countries increased from an average of almost 14 percent of GDP to 25 percent.[16] As Chart 4 illustrates, the expenditure ratio increased in a similar fashion in each of these countries.[17] The pattern of growth, both over time and between programs, however, has varied among countries. On average, the income elasticity of social expenditure—the growth rate of nominal social expenditure relative to the growth rate of nominal GDP—fell from 1.9 for the period 1960–75 to 1.4 for the period 1975–81. But the United Kingdom was the only country where the change in the income elasticity was of this order (also see Table 18). The income

[16] OECD, *Social Expenditure: 1960–1990, Problems of Growth and Control* (1985).

[17] This study and that of the OECD are not based on the same data. However, the differences are not large for the base year, nor do they exhibit any discernible pattern. This is not surprising. This study relies upon official government sources and the definitions of expenditure by category adopted by each. The OECD imposes a consistent accounting framework on these same data. This requires some redefinition and recategorization of expenditures in ways that differ among countries (Table 17).

elasticity of social expenditure increased in France and Japan, indicating that the expenditure ratio rose faster in the second period of slower economic growth, fell slightly in Italy, and fell sharply in Canada, the Federal Republic of Germany, and the United States. In the United States, the expenditure ratio was the same in 1981 as in 1975, while in Canada and the Federal Republic of Germany, the elasticity of less than unity in 1975–81 indicates that the expenditure ratio was actually lower in 1981 than in 1975.

Similarly, in terms of the expenditure ratios for the different programs, there has been, on average, a long-run shift from expenditure on education to expenditure on medical care and pensions. However, this average experience is exemplified by that of Japan, the only country where such a shift has occurred. Elsewhere, the proportion of social expenditure devoted to education fell only in the United Kingdom and the United States, the proportion devoted to medical care increased everywhere except in the United Kingdom, and the proportion devoted to pensions increased only in Italy, Japan, and the United Kingdom. For each program, the ratio of social expenditure to GDP still increased (see Table 18).

What have been the sources of growth in social expenditure? The OECD's study addresses this issue by breaking down the growth rate of nominal social expenditure into five components: (1) general inflation; (2) cost increases in excess of general inflation (the relative price effect); (3) demographic shifts (viz., changes in the size of population groups deemed relevant to particular sectors)[18]; (4) changes in program coverage, reflecting changes in eligibility and utilization; and (5) changes in average real benefits.[19]

Table 1 decomposes the past growth of the government social expenditure of the seven major industrial countries. Without significant exception across programs and countries, the principal source of real growth has been increases in average real benefits: medical benefits per covered person, education outlays per student, and the purchasing power of cash benefits. The impact of changes in coverage has been relatively small, particularly over the 1975–81 period. The fall in coverage under unemployment compensation programs, given rapidly increasing unemployment, may appear anomalous, but it simply reflects the increasing proportion of unemployed persons (youth, women, the long-term unemployed) who were not covered by unemployment compensation. In addition to unemployment compensation, the demographic impact has been relatively strong in the case of pensions, although much smaller overall.

In medical care and education, increases in relative prices have contributed significantly to expenditure growth. Of course, a major source of nominal expenditure growth—and by far the major source in the later period—has been general inflation. But inflation has exactly the same impact on nominal GDP and does not affect the ratio of social expenditure to GDP.[20]

Methodology for Projecting Social Expenditure

The growth-accounting framework used by the OECD in characterizing the forces underlying the past growth in social expenditure provides a basis for the projections in this study, although the requirements of the long-term projections being attempted call for some consolidation and simplification. By definition, the volume of expenditure associated with a particular social program is the product of the number of people benefiting from that program and the average real benefit (in volume terms) that each receives. If the average real benefit is held constant, real volume rises in line with the number of beneficiaries. Because the focus of this paper is on long-term demographic developments, an attempt is made to identify this pure demographic effect on expenditure for each social program and on total social expenditure. This is equivalent to the combined effect of growth in the size of the population group relevant to a particular program and changes in the proportion of the relevant population receiving program benefits.

The detailed demographic projections described in Chapter III provide the basis for the projection of the number of program beneficiaries. For the most part, coverage in the future is assumed to remain at the 1980 rate—the proportion of the relevant population

[18] The "relevant" population groups used to estimate the demographic effect for the different sectors were: (1) health and medical care: the total population; (2) pensions: the population aged 65 and over; (3) unemployment compensation: the number of unemployed; and (4) education: the population aged 0–24.

[19] In the OECD analysis, the growth in average real benefits is computed as a residual. As such, it is a more complicated concept than these descriptions convey. For example, the growth of average real benefits in medical care and education reflect changes in the age composition of the "relevant" population group. In the case of medical care, where the relevant population group is the total population, an aging of the population would be characterized as a change in average benefits rather than as a demographic effect; in education, a shift in the student population toward a greater number of children in the higher age groups would similarly be characterized as a growth in average benefits rather than a demographic effect. In the present study, these shifts in the age composition of beneficiary groups are included within the demographic effects and are treated separately from increases in average benefits; moreover, demographic effects are estimated by taking into account as much as possible the age-specific expenditure patterns within the countries.

[20] This is true in an ex post accounting sense. It is not being asserted that, historically, the growth of real benefits and GDP has been independent of the underlyng inflation rate.

Table 1. Decomposition of the Average Growth Rate of Government Social Expenditure, 1960–75 and 1975–81

	Initial Expenditure Ratio	Nominal Expen-diture	GDP Deflator	Deflated Expen-diture	Relative Prices	Real Expen-diture	Of Which: Demog-raphy	Cover-age	Average real benefit	Final Expenditure Ratio
	1960			*Annual growth rates (percent): 1960–75*						*1975*
Education[1]	3.4	14.7	5.7	8.5	2.2	6.2	0.6	1.4	4.1	5.8
Medical care	2.5	16.7	5.7	10.4	1.3	9.0	1.0	1.3	6.5	5.2
Pensions	4.8	14.1	5.7	7.9	−0.3	8.2	2.4	1.8	3.8	7.3
Unemployment compensation[1]	0.5	18.9	5.7	12.4	−0.3	12.7	4.4	1.5	6.4	1.1
Total of above programs	11.2	15.1	5.7	8.9	0.8	8.0	1.6	1.6	4.6	19.4
Total social expenditure	*13.7*	*14.5*	*5.7*	*8.3*	*0.7*	*7.5*	—	—	—	*23.1*
	1975			*Annual growth rates (percent): 1975–81*						*1981*
Education	5.8	12.5	9.5	2.7	1.3	1.4	−0.4	0.4	1.4	5.7
Medical care	5.2	14.3	9.5	4.4	1.0	3.4	0.5	0.1	2.8	5.6
Pensions	7.3	17.0	9.5	6.8	—	6.8	2.1	1.1	3.5	8.8
Unemployment compensation	1.1	15.7	9.5	5.7	—	5.7	6.5	−2.9	2.2	1.2
Total of above programs	19.4	14.9	9.5	4.9	0.7	4.2	1.2	0.4	2.6	21.3
Total social expenditure	*23.1*	*14.2*	*9.5*	*4.3*	*0.4*	*3.9*	—	—	—	*24.8*

Source: OECD, *Social Expenditure: 1960–1990, Problems of Growth and Control* (1985).
[1] Excluding France.

eligible for benefits and the proportion of those eligible who utilize a program remaining roughly constant. It varies only to the extent that certain strong trends in coverage, or already legislated changes in coverage for particular countries, are taken into account.

Before considering the assumptions that might be made about the growth of average real benefits, it should be realized that even if the *volume* of expenditure grows at the same rate as real GDP, nominal social expenditure can form an increasing proportion of nominal GDP. This is true because unbalanced productivity growth may lead to a rise in the cost of public sector output relative to a rise in the cost of private sector output (a tendency referred to as a relative price effect (Baumol (1967)). In the case of medical care and education, the size of the relative price effect tends to be measured by reference to changes in the appropriate expenditure deflator as compared with changes in the GDP deflator. However, such a comparison can be misleading since the expenditure deflator tends to be an input price deflator, which may be a poor guide to the change in the corresponding output prices.[21]

Projections of expenditure clearly require assumptions to be made about the future growth of average real benefits and relative prices.[22] Since such assumptions are necessarily tentative, no precision is lost by making a single assumption about the growth rate of average benefits for each program—this assumption reflecting changes in both volumes per recipient and relative prices. In medical care and education, these assumptions are particularly speculative, and the reasonableness of the assumptions used can only be judged by reference to the growth in average benefits in the recent past. For example, account should be taken of a wide range of factors affecting the supply of, and demand for, medical care, particularly relating to improvements in medical technology.

For pension benefits, current program provisions (taking into account recently legislated changes) provide a basis for projecting the growth rate of average benefits. In general, such programs provide for increases in benefits to reflect either changes in the cost of living or average earnings (or some combination of both). Furthermore, retirement pension programs have yet to reach maturity in some countries and average benefits will increase as programs develop. The growth in average benefits, over and above general inflation, can either be fairly accurately modeled by using actuarial studies produced by the individual countries or closely approximated.

[21] See Beck (1981) for a discussion of the impact of unbalanced productivity growth on public expenditure growth in the major industrial countries. A large part of social expenditure takes the form of pure transfers. Nevertheless, if the volume of expenditure on transfers (normally measured by deflating nominal expenditure by the consumer price index) grows at the same rate as real GDP, the ratio of nominal social expenditure to nominal GDP can still increase. This tendency is also referred to as a relative price effect.

[22] All the expenditure projections that follow are therefore defined in relation to general price inflation. This expenditure concept is referred to as "real" expenditure. This terminology contrasts with that used by the OECD, which treats real expenditure as a pure volume concept. What is referred to here as "real expenditure" is termed "deflated expenditure" in OECD (1985).

The detailed assumptions in the study are discussed in the chapters dealing with the individual social programs (Chapters IV through VII). It is presumed that no major structural changes will occur in social programs, except those resulting from legislation already enacted.

Methodology for Projecting Economic Growth

In attempting to project the ratio of social expenditure to GDP through the first quarter of the next century, assumptions must be made not only in regard to the evolution of social expenditure, but also in regard to future economic growth. The latter will reflect changes in employment and changes in output per worker. As a result of the demographic developments described in Chapter III, the population of working age will increase through 2025 in most countries. The only country in which this is not the case is the Federal Republic of Germany, although the projected increase is small in Italy, Japan, and the United Kingdom. These developments will affect the labor force and employment, the links to the former being participation rates and to the latter unemployment rates.

Participation rates are assumed to remain close to those currently observed in the labor force. Some allowance has been made for continuing trends toward increasing female participation, increasing higher education enrollments, and a lower retirement age, although not in all countries. In the United States, it is expected that changes in pension policy already enacted will reverse the current trend toward early retirement after 2000, and this is taken into account. Combination of the demographic developments from the baseline scenarios and the participation rate projections yields the growth rates of the labor force shown in the first column of Table 2. These growth rates differ little from the corresponding growth rates of the working-age population. They range from −0.5 percent in the Federal Republic of Germany to 0.6 percent in the United States. With the exception of Canada, which is also at the top end of the range, the other growth rates are positive but small.

In all seven countries it is assumed that there will eventually be some retreat from the recent peak rates of unemployment, with a tendency toward stabilization at rates close to those experienced in the late 1970s or early 1980s. Only in Italy is the baseline unemployment rate projected for 2025 higher than that experienced in 1980, while only in France is it substantially below the 1980 rate. These two cases may seem out of line with what is assumed to happen elsewhere.[23] However, it should be noted that the growth rate of employment is dominated by demographic developments and is not very sensitive to what is assumed about the future unemployment rate. Table 2 shows that, in all but two countries, the rates of employment and labor force growth are identical, while in those two—France and the United States—the rate of employment growth is only marginally higher.

With the exception of France, the Federal Republic of Germany, and the United Kingdom, productivity growth in the baseline scenario is assumed to rise above the rates experienced over the past decade.[24] However, as Table 3 shows, in these three countries

[23] The fact that they are out of line should not be taken to imply that they are any less reasonable. Indeed, the reasonableness of any projection of the unemployment rate 40 years from now is almost impossible to judge.

[24] Unlike the other countries, for the United Kingdom an assumption is made about the future growth rate of real GDP, so that the productivity assumptions are in fact endogenous, given projected employment growth (Mansur (1985)).

Table 2. Labor Market Developments as Projected in the Baseline Scenarios, 1980–2025

(In percent)

Country	Labor Force Growth	Unemployment Rate				Employment Growth
				2025		
	Average annual growth rate	1980	1984	Baseline scenario	Pessimistic economic scenario	Average annual growth rate
Canada	0.5	7.5	11.2	6.0	9.0	0.5
France	0.3	6.3	9.7	2.5	7.0	0.4
Germany, Fed. Rep. of	−0.5	3.0	8.6	3.0	4.0	−0.5
Italy	0.1	7.5	10.2	9.4	9.7	0.1
Japan	0.2	2.0	2.7	2.0	3.0	0.2
United Kingdom	0.1	6.9	13.2	6.0	6.0[1]	0.1
United States	0.6	7.0	7.4	5.5	6.2	0.7

Sources: OECD, *Economic Outlook*, various issues; and Fund staff estimates.

[1] Official United Kingdom projections assume a long-term unemployment rate of 6 percent under all growth scenarios.

Table 3. Productivity and GDP Growth as Projected in the Baseline Scenarios, 1980–2025
(Average annual growth rates in percent)

	Productivity Growth			GDP Growth			
		1980–2025			Baseline scenario		
Country	1974–84	Baseline scenario	Pessimistic economic scenario	1974–84	1980–2000	2000–2010	2010–2025
Canada	0.5	1.5	1.1	2.6	2.8	1.9	1.3
France	2.2	2.0	2.0	2.0	2.5	2.5	2.1
Germany, Fed. Rep. of	2.4	2.0[1]	1.5[1]	1.7	1.5	1.4	1.1
Italy	1.1	2.2	1.7	1.8	2.1	2.4	2.5
Japan	2.6	3.0	2.0	3.6	3.7	2.8	2.8
United Kingdom	1.6	1.4[2]	0.9[2]	1.1	1.5	1.5	1.5
United States	0.3	1.6	1.2	2.2	2.7	2.1	1.9

Sources: OECD, *Economic Outlook*, various issues; and Fund staff estimates.
[1] 1985–2025.
[2] Derived from assumed GDP growth rates and projected employment growth rates.

and Japan, the declines are small. In Canada, Italy, and the United States, a significant productivity improvement is projected. In the first two cases the improvement appears of a reasonable magnitude in light of the very recent deterioration in productivity. The figures for the United States are high by the standards of any period in recent history, but they are taken from official government projections.[25]

The employment growth rates reported in Table 2 are averages for the entire projection period. Because the age structure of the population is not projected to change steadily, labor force and employment growth rates will vary over time. This fact is reflected in the subperiod GDP growth rates shown in Table 3. These are the product of the corresponding subperiod employment growth rates and recent and projected productivity growth rates. The projected average GDP growth rate for the seven major industrial countries is 2.4 percent for 1980–2000, 2.1 percent for 2000–2010, and 1.9 percent for 2010–2025. Thus, on average, projected demographic developments are expected to drive down growth rates from the current average of about 3 percent (for the first half of 1985) to below the 1974–84 average of about 2 percent.

The pattern of growth rates will remain broadly similar to that experienced over the 1974–84 period. The only notable differences are the much improved economic performance in France and Italy (the former a result of increasing employment and the latter the result of productivity improvement), and the much lower GDP growth in Canada (the result of a marked fall in the labor force growth rate) despite improved productivity. Note also that real growth falls in Japan and the United States as employment growth slows.

The social expenditure scenarios elaborated in later chapters and the economic growth scenarios described above combine with the initial expenditure ratios presented in Table 15 to yield projections of future government social expenditure ratios. These scenarios are interrelated. For example, the growth in average benefits is generally related to the growth of income in the economy as a whole—either per capita GDP or average productivity—and the expenditure on unemployment compensation programs is a function of the assumed rate of unemployment. However, no explicit effects from social expenditure relate to economic growth, except insofar as future participation rates have been revised to reflect changes in retirement age. Thus, output is not related to the level of medical care, education, or pension benefits.[26]

Nor is there any link between the scenarios across countries. Of course, links are only likely to exist in the case of the social expenditure scenarios to the extent that economic developments may impose a need for restrictions on the growth of social expenditure and to the extent that economic developments are themselves linked. The failure to take explicit account of international linkages between the economies of the seven major industrial countries is unlikely to be a serious omission given the large element of common experience characterizing their long-term scenarios and the slow rates of change implied.

[25] United States, Board of Trustees of the OASDI Trust Funds (1984).

[26] This serves to emphasize the fact that the study presents expenditure *projections* rather than predictions. In the latter case, an attempt would be made to model the impact of policy responses to increasing expenditure (both those designed to control expenditure growth and those designed to increase the capacity of the economy to finance it).

The social expenditure and economic growth scenarios could also be linked more directly through the aging process itself. Future expenditure on medical care, education, pensions, and other benefits respond to the aging of the population. The channels through which these responses occur, and their extent, emerge clearly from the social expenditure projections. Future economic growth also responds to aging of the population, but this factor emerges in the projections only as a change in the size of the labor force. However, as shown in Chapter III, when the population ages over the next 40 years, so does the labor force. Yet no attempt has been made to explore the economic implications of an aging labor force, and in particular, the relationship between average age and average productivity. While it seems likely that these factors are related, productivity may be influenced more by technological developments and other changes in working practices—relationships which also remain unexplored.

III Population Dynamics in the Seven Major Industrial Countries

A significant change is projected in the demographic structure of the seven major industrial countries over the next several decades. Through the year 2000 much of this change can be predicted with reasonable certainty, since changes in demographic parameters are not likely to offset the impact of the movement of existing population cohorts through the age structure. Looking beyond the turn of the century, unanticipated changes in fertility rates or life expectancies may influence the age structure of the population. This chapter reviews current demographic projections for the seven major industrial countries, examines their underlying determinants, and briefly explores their sensitivity to more extreme demographic assumptions.

Demographic projections are routinely carried out in most industrial countries, either in connection with census work or for actuarial analyses of the financing of public pension schemes. Almost always, countries make several projections, examining the effects of alternative demographic scenarios. In this study the "baseline" projections have, in most cases, been chosen so that their demographic parameters closely correspond to the "middle" demographic projections made by the country concerned. The exception is Japan, where the official projections would indicate a slightly more rapid aging of the population. For all countries, an alternative "greater aging" scenario is examined, corresponding to a situation of lower fertility rates and more rapid improvements in life expectancy.[27]

Underlying Demographic Assumptions

The baseline scenarios for the seven countries are built on the assumption of a gradual 8–16 percent increase in the fertility rate from the low levels experienced in 1980 (Chart 5 and Table 19).[28] This implies that by 2010, five of the seven countries will have a fertility rate sufficient ultimately to ensure at least a stable population size (i.e., 2.1). For the Federal Republic of Germany and Italy, fertility rates are assumed to increase but will remain at 1.7 and 1.9, respectively, through the year 2025. It should be recalled that fertility rates above 2 were typical in all the industrial countries through the 1960s, reaching almost 4 in Canada and the United States in 1960. In the mid-1960s, fertility rates were 2.7 or above in Canada, the United Kingdom, and the United States; the lowest rate experienced was about 2.3 in the Federal Republic of Germany and Italy.

Projections of mortality rates are subject to considerable uncertainty, as was clearly indicated in the early 1970s, when demographers in the United States seriously underestimated the improvements in life expectancy that actually took place. The baseline scenario projects further improvements in life expectancy, so that by the year 2025 the average life expectancy of males and females should rise to 74.5 and 80.5, respectively (Chart 5 and Table 19).[29] Such improvements are relatively conservative, compared with those potentially possible from medical breakthroughs. For

[27] The official projections were drawn from the following sources: Canada, Economic Council of Canada (1979); France, Institut National de la Statistique et des Etudes Economiques (1978); Germany (Federal Republic), Bundesregierung (1980); Italy, Istituto di Ricerche sulla Popolazione (1984); Japan, Institute of Population Problems (1982); United Kingdom, Office of Population Censuses and Surveys (1984); Wade (1984); and United States, Board of Trustees of the OASDI Trust Funds (1985). In the case of Japan, the official projections of the share of the elderly are bounded by the two alternative demographic scenarios of this study.

[28] The fertility rate is a measure of the total number of children that would be born to an average woman during her fertile years, if the age-specific fertility rates experienced during the year of measurement continue throughout her fertile life. The fertility rate reflects the influence of the proportion of the population married and the age of marriage, as well as the numerous socioeconomic factors which affect the decision of a woman to bear children (inter alia, the perceived economic cost of bearing children). For the industrial countries (with low rates of infant mortality), a fertility rate of about 2.1 is, in principle, required for a closed population just to reproduce itself over time.

[29] A slight decline is projected for France; in part, this indicates the extent to which projections can quickly become dated. The French baseline scenario was based on 1978 projections made by the Institut National de la Statistique et des Etudes Economiques (INSEE). The lack of optimism largely reflects the failure of life expectancy to improve in France in recent years, reflecting high mortality from alcohol and tobacco-related illnesses.

Chart 5. Assumed Demographic Parameters, 1980–2025

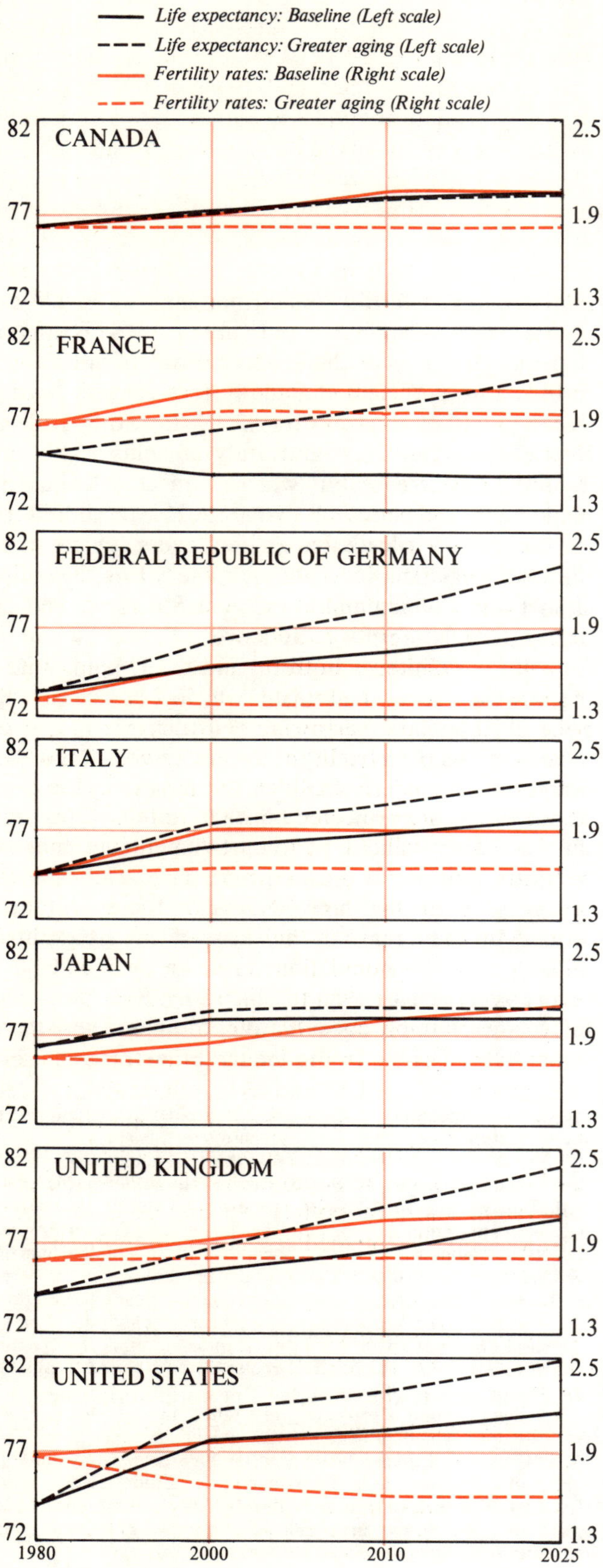

example, in the United States, the baseline scenario assumes an annual improvement of 0.9 percent in mortality over the entire period (though a higher rate of 1.4 percent a year between 1980 and 2000), compared with the 1.7 percent rate experienced during the 1970s. It should be noted that this added longevity will not necessarily be associated with a substantial improvement in the morbidity or disability rates of the very elderly.

Patterns of immigration may also have an important bearing on demographic developments. The assumptions relating to immigration reflect the varying experiences anticipated for the different countries. For example, the baseline scenario for the Federal Republic of Germany assumes net emigration of approximately a million persons in the period 1980–90, with no further net migration in subsequent years. For the United Kingdom, the baseline scenario assumes net emigration of approximately 75,000 a year through 1990, dropping progressively to 15,000 by 2010 and 10,000 by 2015.[30] For Italy, net emigration is assumed to be low and declining over time. In France and Japan, no net migration is assumed. On the other hand, in Canada and the United States, sizable immigration is expected. In Canada, the baseline scenario assumes that immigration will be close to 100,000 persons annually through the end of this century and then will drop to approximately 50,000 a year. In the United States, the baseline scenario assumes net immigration of 400,000 a year.

Principal Results of the Baseline Scenario

Striking differences appear across the Group of Seven in the extent to which they have already experienced a significant change in the age structure of their populations. In four countries—France, the Federal Republic of Germany, Italy, and the United Kingdom—the share of the population aged 65 and over already exceeds 13 percent, with a high of almost 16 percent in the Federal Republic of Germany, in contrast to only 9–11 percent in Canada, Japan, and the United States (Chart 6 and Table 20).

These differences in the share of the elderly principally correspond to differences in the size of the potential working-age population. The share of the young (aged 0–14) in the population is clustered around 22 percent, with only the Federal Republic of Germany being substantially less, at 17 percent. The European

[30] This is slightly higher than the recently issued demographic projections for the United Kingdom (Office of Population Censuses and Surveys, 1984), which assume emigration of approximately 19,000 a year in 1985, declining to 9,000 a year in 1990. The "greater aging" scenario assumes no net migration over the period.

Chart 6. Demographic Structure of the Population, 1980–2025

(In percent)

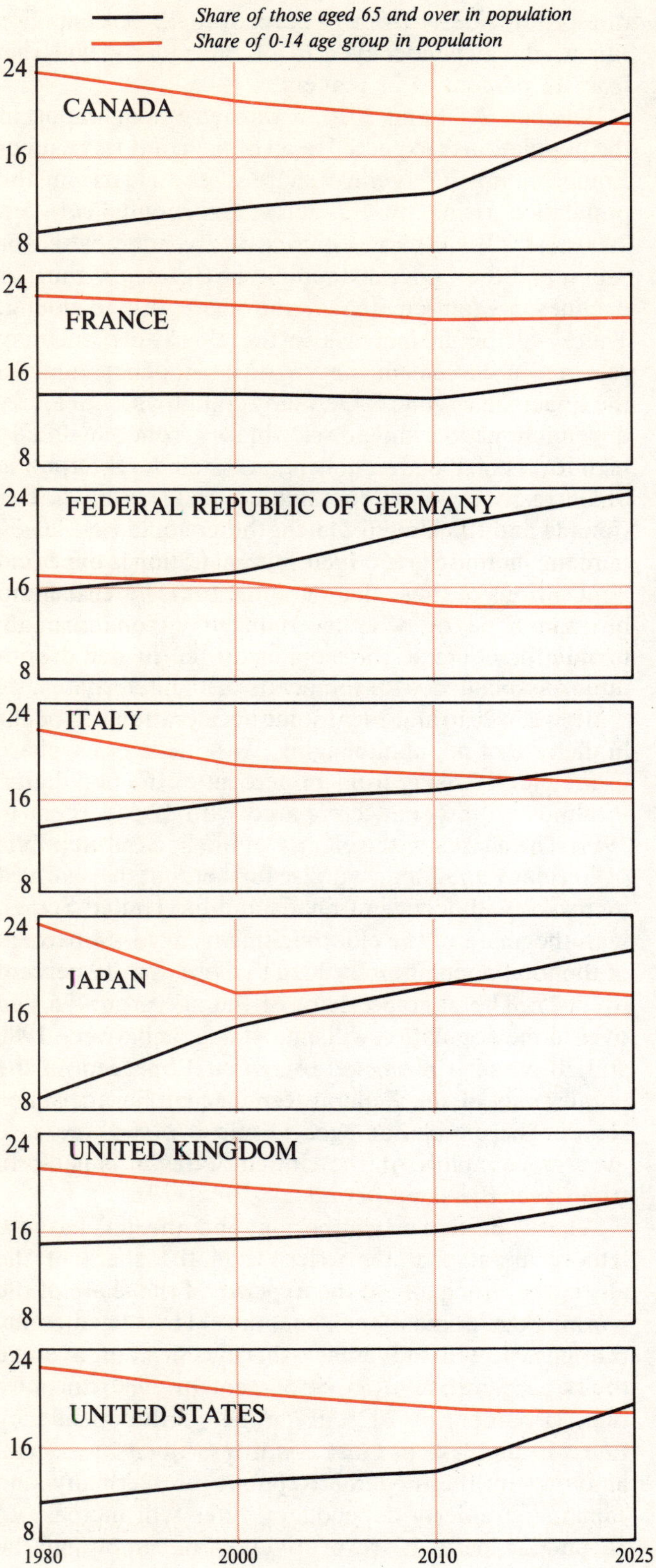

nations reveal a significantly higher elderly dependency rate (Chart 7 and Table 21), with the elderly constituting approximately 21–23 percent of the potential working-age population in 1980 (set for illustrative purposes at age 15–64).[31] In contrast, the elderly dependency rate ranges from 13 to 17 percent in Canada, Japan, and the United States. The youth dependency ratio varies less across countries and is maintained at 33–35 percent (with the exception of the Federal Republic of Germany where it is 25 percent). The share of the very old in the population (those 75 and over) also differs markedly across countries, by as much as a factor of 2, and is particularly high in France, the Federal Republic of Germany, and the United Kingdom (Chart 8 and Table 20).

Through the year 2000, the impact of the largely predictable evolution of the different cohorts through the populations can be observed. The size of particular cohorts is largely determined by past demographic and historical events—baby "booms" and "busts," wars, epidemics, and periods of economic hardship. Changes in the elderly population (65 and over) are a direct function of births 65 years ago and before as well as age-specific net immigration, and are attenuated by age-specific mortality patterns.

What is striking is both the increased aging that is expected to occur in almost all of the countries by the year 2000 and the narrowing of the dispersion in the shares of the elderly. In the countries with the lowest shares of the elderly in 1980, the largest increases in these shares are projected by 2000; in Japan, the share of the elderly will rise by almost 70 percent, primarily reflecting the rapid decline in fertility rates that has occurred over the last 30 years. There will be a concomitant increase in the share of the age group 75 and over in the population: from an average of 1 in every 21 people in 1980 to 1 in 17 by 2000. The share of the population aged 85 and over increases even more dramatically. In the United States, for example, the population aged 85 and over will double between 1984 and 2000 (to 2 percent of the population). The increasing importance of these groups within the elderly segment of the population will have very important ramifications for both the magnitude and character of the demands for medical and institutional nursing services by the elderly.

In most countries, the increase in the share of the age group 65 and over will be *more* than offset by a decrease in the share of the population under age 15. In Japan alone, the share of the population under age 15 will decline from almost 24 percent in 1980 to approximately 18 percent by the year 2000. Thus, both

[31] Since countries differ in both the likely ages of employment and retirement, no age grouping is fully appropriate across countries to define uniformly the potential working-age group.

Chart 7. Dependency Rates, 1980–2025

(In percent)

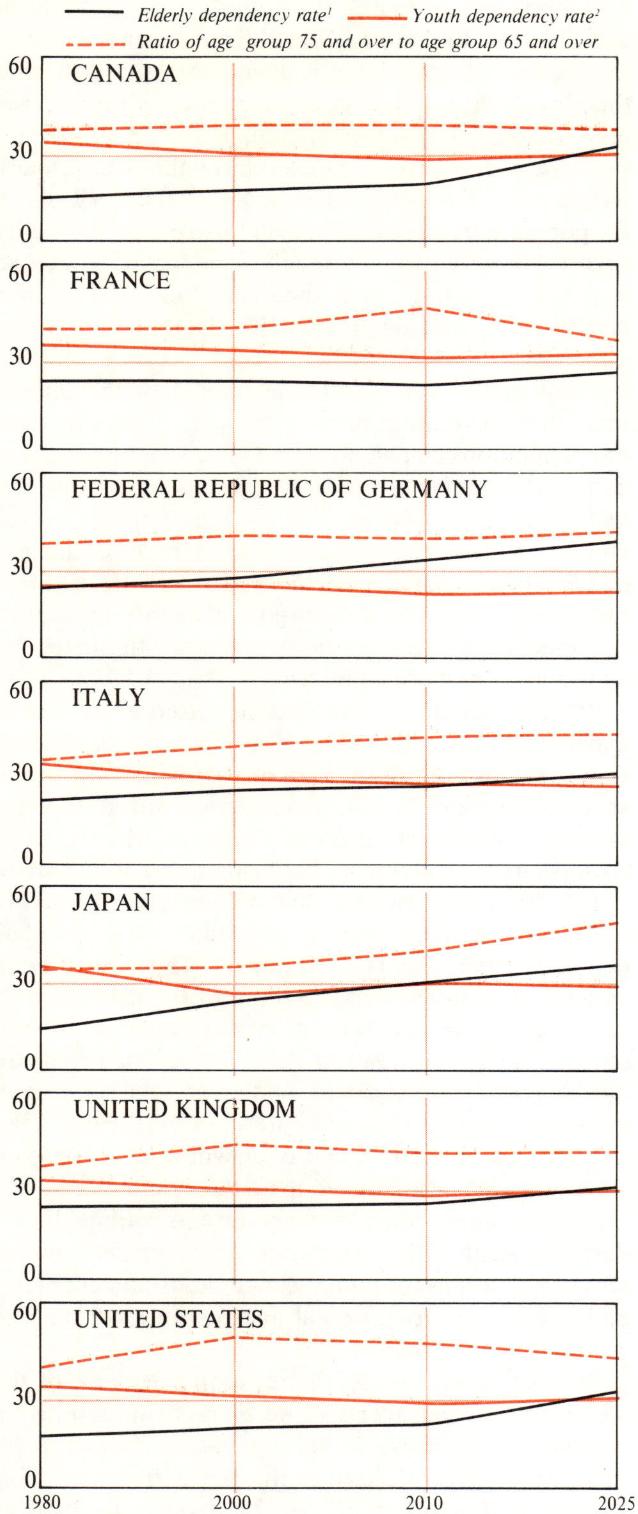

[1] Ratio of population aged 65 and over to population aged 15–64 (in percent).

[2] Ratio of population aged under 15 to population aged 15–64 (in percent).

a decline in the overall dependency rate in all countries (except in the case of the Federal Republic of Germany) and *a shift in the balance between the elderly and the young* will be observed. The average dependency rate of the young will decline from 33 percent to 29 percent and will be almost offset by the increased dependency rate of the elderly from 19 percent to 22 percent. For Japan, the dependency rate of the elderly will rise from 13 percent to 22 percent.

Between 2000 and 2010, a further gradual aging of the population is expected in all of the countries except France, with the average share of the elderly in the population rising by 1.7 percentage points between 2000 and 2010. Sharper increases are anticipated for Japan and the Federal Republic of Germany. Further declines are anticipated in the share of the young. There will be an increase in the elderly dependency rate and a decline in the youth dependency rate. In the Federal Republic of Germany and Japan, the elderly dependency rates should rise sharply from the already high levels of 1980, increasing in the Federal Republic of Germany by 40 percent and doubling in Japan. For Canada and the United States, there would be a 20–30 percent increase over 1980 levels. Clearly, the fiscal implications of these demographic trends are likely to be influenced by whether reduced expenditure demands for education are offset by the higher expenditure associated with the needs of the elderly.

Between 2010 and 2025, some acceleration will occur in the rate of population aging, with the average share of the elderly rising from 16 percent of the population to almost 20 percent, compared with 12.5 percent in 1980. The shares of the elderly in the Federal Republic of Germany and Japan will rise further, but the sharpest increases will occur in Canada and the United States, with the share of the elderly rising from 13–14 percent of the total population by 2010 to more than 19 percent by 2025. The average share of the age group 75 and over in the population will almost double between 1980 and 2025 and is projected to *exceed* 10 percent of the populations of the Federal Republic of Germany and Japan. The population aged 85 and over will increase even more rapidly; in the United States, it is likely to triple over the same period.

What is particularly important about trends in these later years is that the increase in the share of the elderly is principally at the expense of the share of the working-age population. Thus, the elderly dependency rate is expected to increase sharply, from an average of 24 percent by 2010 (19 percent in 1980) to more than 31 percent by 2025. Even the youth dependency rate will increase in most countries, albeit by a small amount. In the Federal Republic of Germany and Japan, the elderly dependency rates will increase to 38 and 35 percent, respectively. Put simply, if the

Chart 8. Share of Age Group 75 and Over in the Population, 1980–2025
(In percent)

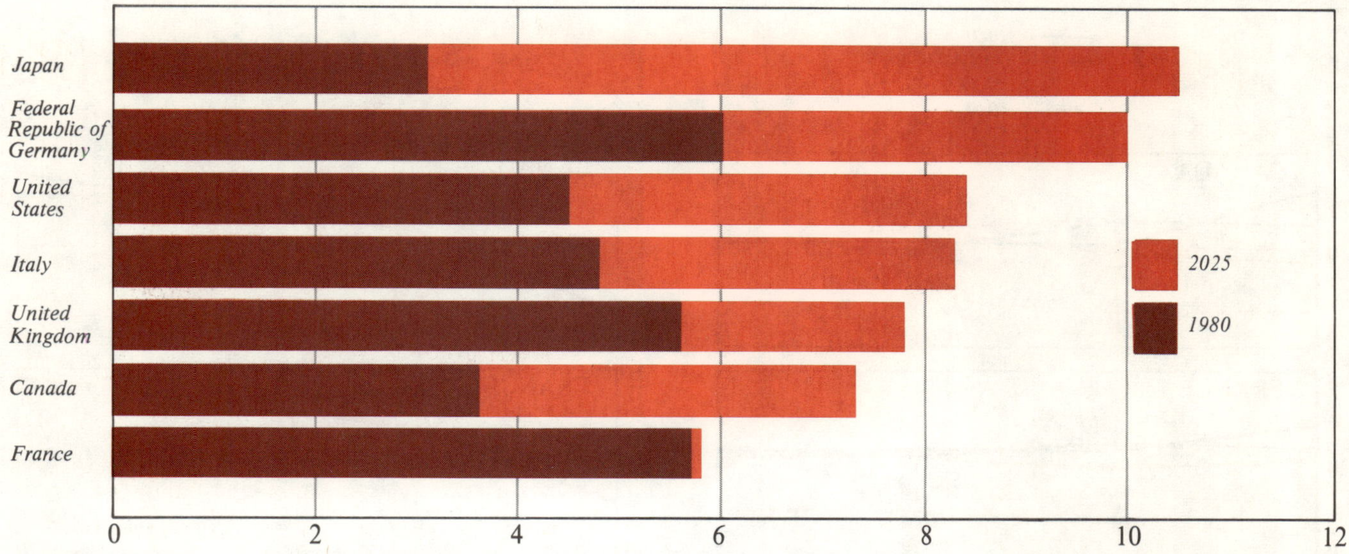

entire group aged 15–64 in the Federal Republic of Germany and Japan were employed, less than three workers would be available to pay for pensions and medical care on a pay-as-you-go basis by 2025, compared with five in 1980.

Several other characteristics of the evolving age structure of the industrial countries should be noted. First, what will most differentiate the next several decades from the preceding two decades is the shift in age composition rather than the rate of increase in the number of elderly. On average, the annual growth rate in the number of elderly in the period 1980–2025 will be only *half* what it was in the preceding two decades (1.3 percent vs. 2.4 percent). However, the rate of total population growth will *shrink* even more sharply (by a factor of almost four), so that the share of the elderly will be rising even more rapidly.

Second, the share of the very old (i.e., 75 and over) among the elderly will rise on average from 38 percent in 1980 to 42 percent by the year 2000. However, in some countries, the increase will be dramatic: in Japan, the group aged 75 and over is expected to rise from a third to half of the elderly population over the whole period.

Third, a striking compositional change will take place in the structure of the population aged 20–64, the principal group in the labor force (Chart 9 and Table 22). By 2000, the share in this group of those aged 20–29 will fall sharply in Canada, France, the Federal Republic of Germany, and the United States. In Canada and the United States, the declining share of this group will be offset by a sharp increase in the share of the group aged 40–49, whereas in the Federal Republic of Germany the shares of those aged 60–64 and, to a lesser extent, the group aged 30–39 will show significant increases. In each subsequent decade, there will be a corresponding movement of these cohorts through the age structure. From 2010, the share of the group aged 20–39 will, on average, begin a decline from 52 percent to 42–44 percent by 2025. The aging of the labor force is likely to have important implications for the growth in productivity, the rate of technological change, the savings-consumption behavior of the population, and many other important socioeconomic variables.

Finally, it is useful to note the expected movement in the absolute size of the overall population of the seven major industrial countries over the period 1980–2025 (Chart 10 and Table 21). At one extreme, current projections suggest a continuous growth, albeit at a decelerating rate, in the populations of Canada and the United States, with more than a 30 percent increase anticipated by the year 2025 over the 1980 level. A similar though lower growth rate is anticipated for France and Japan; however, it is noteworthy that the Japanese population virtually ceases to grow after the year 2010. Italy and the United Kingdom are expected to experience only limited growth in their populations over the entire period, with the Italian population declining during the period 2010–25. In the Federal Republic of Germany, the population is expected to decline continuously throughout the period.

The "Greater Aging" Scenario

Forecasts of social expenditure have also been made on the assumption of lower fertility rates and higher

Chart 9. Age Composition of the Population Aged 20–64, 1980–2025

(As a percentage of the population aged 20–64)

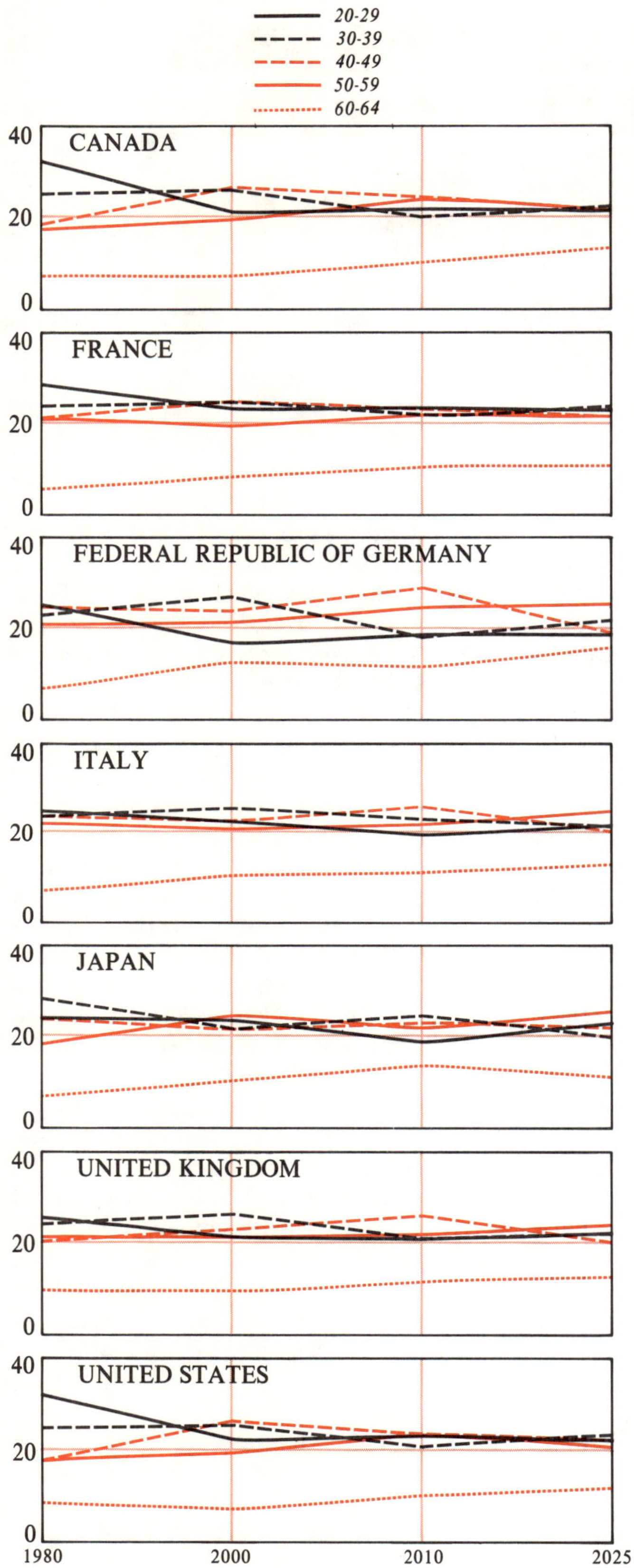

Chart 10. Population Size, 1980–2025

(In millions)

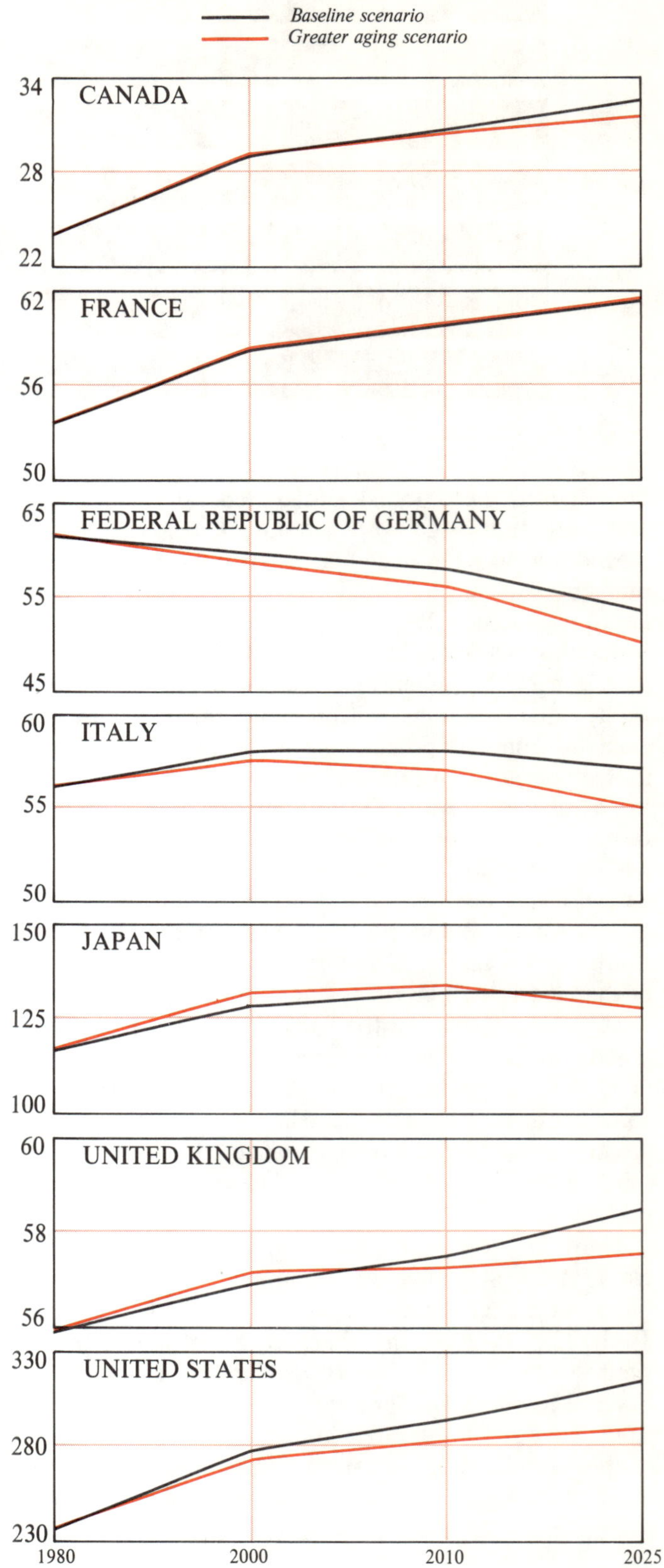

life expectancies, thus yielding "greater aging" in the population. Such an alternative scenario provides a sense of the upper bounds implied by demographic factors in the demand for social expenditure. The alternative demographic assumptions are indicated in Chart 5 and Table 19. For this scenario, fertility rates are assumed to remain at their 1980 level,[32] and life expectancy is projected to improve more rapidly than in the baseline scenario.[33] Lower fertility rates tend to have a slow-acting, but important, cumulative effect on the population size and structure. As persons in the reproductive age groups have smaller numbers of children, this development will be reflected in a smaller size of the reproductive age groups 20 to 30 years later. Lower mortality rates are reflected earlier, both sustaining the size of the elderly group and, over time, becoming more important as the size of the elderly population increases, with the "baby boom" segment moving into the elderly age group.

The alternative demographic assumptions have an impact on the relative shares of the population aged 0–14 and 65 and over by the year 2025. On average, the former group declines from 22 percent of the population in 1980 to almost 15 percent (rather than the 18 percent projected in the baseline scenario); the latter group rises from 12.5 percent in 1980 to 22 percent (rather than the 19.5 percent projected in the baseline scenario). Consequently, while almost no change in the overall dependency rate occurs, there is a further increase (decrease) in the dependency rate of the elderly (youth) population. The share of the population aged 75 and over also rises, from 5 percent in 1980 to 10 percent by 2025 (relative to 8 percent in the baseline scenario), implying a further increase in the share of the very elderly in the population.

In terms of the total population size, the effect of these alternative assumptions is to leave the population either unchanged in size relative to the baseline scenario, or somewhat lower. Italy's population would decline in absolute size by the end of the period, primarily reflecting the cumulative impact of lower fertility rates that take effect after the year 2010. The Federal Republic of Germany's population would contract even further relative to its present size, particularly in the period 2010–25. For the United States, the rate of population growth would be significantly less over the period.

While it is impossible to judge whether technological advances in medicine and sociological factors will coincide to produce the projected combination of demographic patterns, alternative scenarios nevertheless provide a sense of the upper bounds implied by demographic factors in the demand for social expenditure.

[32] For the United States, the "greater aging" scenario reflects the official "pessimistic" scenario of the Social Security Administration, which suggests a decline in the fertility rate from 1.86 to 1.6 over the next 25 years.

[33] This is an improvement in life expectancy of approximately 0.13–0.2 percent a year over the period 1980–2025, compared with an improvement of 0.07–0.1 percent in the baseline scenario.

IV Pensions

The largest single item of social expenditure in most of the seven major industrial countries is pensions; Canada and Japan are the only exceptions (Chart 3 and Table 15). Of the three major government social programs, the pension program has also been the fastest growing.[34] As Table 1 shows, demographic factors, improved program coverage, and benefit increases have all contributed significantly to the growth of real pension expenditure. Benefit increases have tended to be the principal influence on expenditure growth, although demographic changes have had a strong effect, particularly in Japan. As long as populations continue to age, the demographic factor will exert considerable influence on pension expenditure.

Demography and Pension Expenditure

As Chapter III shows, the absolute number of elderly people—those aged 65 and over—is expected to increase in each of the seven major industrial countries. However, changes in the numbers of elderly do not necessarily correspond to changes in the numbers of pensioners. First, the eligibility age for pensions is not 65 in each country; 65 is the maximum "normal" pension age. Appendix II contains a summary of the principal features of the major public pension programs in each of the seven countries, including normal pension age and average benefit levels (Table 33). The evolution of the numbers of people of pension age can be derived from the demographic projections described in Chapter III (see upper half of Table 4). For the most part, the growth in the number of people of pension age and the growth in the number of elderly are the same. One exception is France, where the number of people aged 60–64 is projected to grow faster than the number of people aged 65 and over. The other exception is Japan, where the number of people aged 60–64 is projected to grow more slowly than the number of people aged 65 and over.

Second, changes in the number of elderly (or changes in the number of people of pension age) do not correspond to changes in the number of pensioners because pension programs typically permit some flexibility in actual retirement age (with a corresponding adjustment to pensions). The lower half of Table 4 reflects the actual patterns of retirement age.[35] For most countries, the two halves of the table differ little. In the Federal Republic of Germany, the somewhat faster growth in the number of pensioners reflects past increases in labor force participation, particularly among females, and a continuing trend toward early retirement. In the United States, an allowance has been made for a phased increase in the pension age from 65 to 67 between 2000 and 2025. In Japan, the number of pensioners is roughly equal to the number of people aged 55 and over, rather than the number of people

Table 4. Growth in the Number of People of Pension Age and Numbers of Pensioners, as Projected in the Baseline Scenarios, 1980–2025

(Index 1980 = 100)

Country	1980	2000	2010	2025
	(Index of number of people of pension age)[1]			
Canada	100	142	169	272
France	100	118	128	147
Germany, Fed. Rep. of	100	112	128	138
Italy	100	123	132	148
Japan	100	178	226	238
United Kingdom	100	103	109	130
United States	100	136	153	230
	(Index of number of retirement pensioners)			
Canada	100	142	169	272
France	100	122	132	150
Germany, Fed. Rep. of	100	134	155	170
Italy	100	122	130	144
Japan	100	172	206	215
United Kingdom	100	103	109	130
United States	100	136	150	215

Source: Fund staff estimates.

[1] Pension ages (men/women) are assumed to be: Canada—65/65; France—60/60; Federal Republic of Germany—63/63; Italy—60/55; Japan—60/60; United Kingdom—65/60; and United States—65/65.

[34] Expenditure on unemployment compensation programs has grown faster, especially in Europe. The extent, timing, and sources of this growth are described in Chapter VII.

[35] In Canada and the United Kingdom, all persons over pension age is assumed to be retired.

aged 60 and over, and for the purposes of the projection this is treated as a long-term equality. This age group (55 and over) will, in turn, grow more slowly than the number of people aged 60 and over. Third, the number of pensioners is not only affected by retirement but also by the number of people who receive general non-retirement pensions (e.g., disability pensions).

Across countries, considerable variation is seen in the growth of the numbers of pensioners. At the extremes, the growth rate in Canada is more than twice that of the United Kingdom. Japan and the United States exhibit the same long-term growth rate, which is exceeded only, and substantially, in Canada. But the patterns of growth are markedly different. In Japan, 63 percent of the total increase occurs before 2000; in the United States, 56 percent of the total increase occurs after 2010. In Canada, 61 percent of the total increase occurs after 2010; the corresponding figure is 70 percent in the United Kingdom. Elsewhere, the growth in the number of pensioners is moderate and steady.

Given prospective numbers of pensioners, future pension expenditure is determined by the average pension that each one receives. If this latter factor is held constant, then an index of the number of pensioners would also be an index of real pension expenditure. Indeed, in that it shows how real pension expenditure changes as a result of increases in the number of pensioners alone, it represents a pure demographic effect. However, average pensions are unlikely to remain constant in real terms.

Pension Expenditure Projections, 1980–2025

There are a number of reasons why average pensions will increase in real terms over time. First, in some countries full pension rights are conferred only on people who retire after having spent a considerable part, if not all, of their working life in a program. If newly retired pensioners benefit, relative to their predecessors, from having been in a program for a greater part of their working life—because longer membership necessarily implies a bigger pension—then that program can still be viewed as immature. The more immature a program, the greater the difference or the longer it will take to close the gap between current and long-term real pension levels for newly retired pensioners.[36] Second, initial pensions are often related directly to past earnings, and to the extent that real earnings grow over time, so do initial pension levels. And third, there are generally provisions for regular post-retirement pension increases. Often these provisions do no more than compensate for increases in the cost of living, so that real pensions remain constant. But in some countries pensions are indexed to earnings even after retirement, and an increase in real earnings will again imply an increase in real pension levels.

In each of the seven major industrial countries, the principal social security programs pay earnings-related pensions, or a combination of flat-rate and earnings-related pensions (Canada, Japan, and the United Kingdom). Post-retirement increases are related to gross earnings in France, net-of-tax earnings in the Federal Republic of Germany, a combination of earnings and cost of living in Italy, and prices or cost of living elsewhere. The programs in Canada, Italy, Japan, the United Kingdom, and the United States are, to varying degrees, immature.

Intercountry differences in the structure of social security programs have to be modeled in order to project average real pension benefits. The indices of real pension expenditure reported in Table 5 reflect these differences, which are described in more detail in Appendix II. They also incorporate expenditure on survivors' and disability pensions and, in some cases, pensions paid to public sector employees (see Appendix II for details). In comparison with the index

Table 5. Indices of the Growth in Real Pension Expenditure and the Ratio of Pension Expenditure to GDP, as Projected in the Baseline Scenarios, 1980–2025

(Index 1980 = 100)

Country	1980	2000	2010	2025
	(Index of real pension expenditure)			
Canada	100	154	189	317
France	100	175	230	325
Germany, Fed. Rep. of	100	180	218	300
Italy	100	198	285	498
Japan	100	430	787	1,314
United Kingdom	100	159	199	290
United States	100	145	178	306
	(Index of the ratio of pension expenditure to GDP)			
Canada	100	89	89	123
France	100	110	115	130
Germany, Fed. Rep. of	100	129	140	154
Italy	100	121	138	171
Japan	100	229	307	319
United Kingdom	100	115	124	144
United States	100	92	90	110

Source: Fund staff estimates.

[36] Defining immaturity in terms of the pensions received by newly retired pensioners ignores the impact of immaturity as reflected in the pensions received by older pensioners. Only if maturity is defined in terms of the pensions paid on retirement to *all pensioners* would this be taken into account. A program will be mature when every retired person has accrued the maximum potential pension possible under the scheme, given his or her earnings.

numbers reflecting the pure demographic effect (Table 4), those in Canada and the United States increase least, as there is no significant maturation effect and pensions are adjusted in line only with prices after retirement (i.e., they are fixed in real terms).[37] Pensions of the newly retired in these two countries are adjusted in line with earnings (except the flat-rate component in Canada), which are assumed to grow with average productivity, and that is why the index numbers increase faster than those reflecting pure demographic changes.

More immature programs are found in Italy, Japan, and the United Kingdom. In Italy, pensions are assumed to increase with earnings, plus an additional 0.5 percent to reflect immaturity. Since post-retirement indexation reflects a combination of earnings and price changes, the excess of growth in line with earnings plus 0.5 percent over expected pre-retirement and post-retirement growth reflects the impact of increasing maturity on average pension levels. In Japan and the United Kingdom, earnings-related pensions increase in line with prices after retirement and flat-rate pensions increase in line with prices. However, for Japan, it is assumed that the average pension grows at 1.5 percentage points more than the growth in GDP per capita up until 2010, by which time the average replacement rate should be close to its maximum level under the recently enacted pension law.[38]

For the United Kingdom, the development of the State Earnings Related Pension Scheme (SERPS) has been modeled explicitly in the official United Kingdom projections which underlie the indices in Table 5; however, in this projection both flat-rate and earnings-related pensions, after retirement, are assumed to increase at the same rate as GDP per capita and the projections have been amended to reflect the impact of recent reforms.[39] In these three countries, average real benefits are set to grow most rapidly, and considerably more so in Japan than elsewhere.

In France and the Federal Republic of Germany, the pre-retirement pension base and post-retirement pension increases are kept in line with earnings. In the Federal Republic of Germany, increases after retirement have recently been switched from a gross to a net earnings basis. This change is reflected in the projections.

[37] The projections for the United States are drawn from United States, Board of Trustees of the OASDI Trust Funds (1985).

[38] This assumption is fairly arbitrary, as there are no official projections for the public pension system as a whole. However, this assumption produces the intended results of the 1985 Pension Reform Act discussed further in the text and Appendix II.

[39] The official projections are contained in United Kingdom, *National Insurance Fund Long-Term Financial Estimates* (1982). The recent reforms to SERPS are described in the text and Appendix II.

While real pension expenditure is increasing, the real income of the working population may be increasing at the same time. The pension burden—the proportion of its income the working population must give up to pay pensions to the retired—need not increase. In Chapter III it is shown that, with the exception of the Federal Republic of Germany, the population of working age is going to increase. Naturally, not everybody of working age is employed. Chapter II describes the participation rate and unemployment rate assumptions used in the study for projections of future employment. It also reports the productivity growth assumptions that combine with the employment projections to yield the estimates of future GDP. Comparisons of future pension expenditure and future GDP reveal whether the pension burden will increase or decrease.

Table 5 reports indices of the ratio of pension expenditure to GDP, which take into account projected GDP growth in the baseline scenario, as indicated in Table 3. The offset this provides to real expenditure growth is clearly greatest in Japan, of a lesser but still considerable order of magnitude in Canada, France, Italy, and the United States, and significant even in the slow-growing countries (the Federal Republic of Germany and the United Kingdom). Thus, across countries, pension ratios will more than triple in Japan, increase between 50 percent and 100 percent in the Federal Republic of Germany and Italy, and increase by less than 50 percent in Canada, France, the United Kingdom, and the United States. In Canada and the United States, the ratio will fall before 2010 and increase after 2010. The increase in the pension ratio will also occur more strongly after 2010 in France, Italy, and the United Kingdom, and it will be steadier in the Federal Republic of Germany and Japan, although it should be noted that in Japan the pension ratio more than doubles before 2000.

It is interesting to compare these prospective developments with those of the past (Table 6). In Chapter III, it is pointed out that the number of elderly people will grow more slowly in the future than it has in the past, and the same is true of real pension expenditure. Indeed, the lowest growth rate recorded over the 1960–80 period (4.8 percent in the United Kingdom) is only slightly over 1 percentage point lower than the highest growth rate projected over the 1980–2025 period (5.9 percent in Japan). The growth in the pension ratio is also much lower than it has been in the past, despite assumed GDP growth rates that are also low by historical standards. The problem is, of course, at least in some countries, that the ratio of pension expenditure to GDP is already high, and it may be heading toward a level which future working generations will judge unacceptable.

Table 6. Annual Growth Rate of Real Pension Expenditure and of the Ratio of Government Pension Expenditure to GDP in Historical Perspective, 1960–80 and 1980–2025

	Annual Growth Rate of:			
	Real pension expenditure		Ratio of pension expenditure to GDP	
Country	1960–80	1980–2025	1960–80	1980–2025
Canada	7.2	2.6	2.4	0.5
France	8.2	2.7	3.4	0.6
Germany, Fed. Rep. of	4.9	2.5	1.2	1.0
Italy	8.5	3.6	4.3	1.2
Japan	14.1	5.9	6.0	2.6
United Kingdom	4.8	2.4	2.9	0.8
United States	6.2	2.5	2.7	0.2

Sources: OECD, *Social Expenditure: 1960–1990, Problems of Growth and Control* (1985); and Fund staff estimates.

Thus far the projections have been presented in the form of index numbers. Therefore, this discussion of population aging, future pension expenditure, and the pension ratio has not been influenced by differences between countries in the ratio of pension expenditure to GDP. These differences have been very wide in the past (Chart 11 and Table 14). In part, this reflects definitional variations, although the differences are still wide even with a much larger measure of international comparability (Table 16). They will also remain so in the future, as Chart 11 shows. This chart has been derived by applying the index numbers describing the growth of the pension ratio in Table 5 to the 1980 expenditure ratios (see Table 14 for precise statistics).

Across the seven major industrial countries, the pension expenditure implications of population aging in Canada and the United States—with low expenditure ratios increasing very modestly—are not serious. In France and the United Kingdom, the outlook is worse; in the first case, because the expenditure ratio is already high, and in the second case, because expenditure will increase significantly. In Japan, the expenditure ratio is currently low, but it will be among the highest by 2025. However, the outlook is clearly bleakest in the Federal Republic of Germany and Italy, where the combination of high initial expenditure ratios and relatively rapid growth will produce ratios of expenditure to GDP of over 20 percent by 2025.

Alternative Demographic and Economic Scenarios

Alternative scenarios described in earlier chapters focus on what happens if the demographic situation and/or the economy are less favorable than in the baseline scenario. Chart 11 indicates the effect of

Chart 11. Government Pension Expenditure as Percentage of GDP, 1980–2025

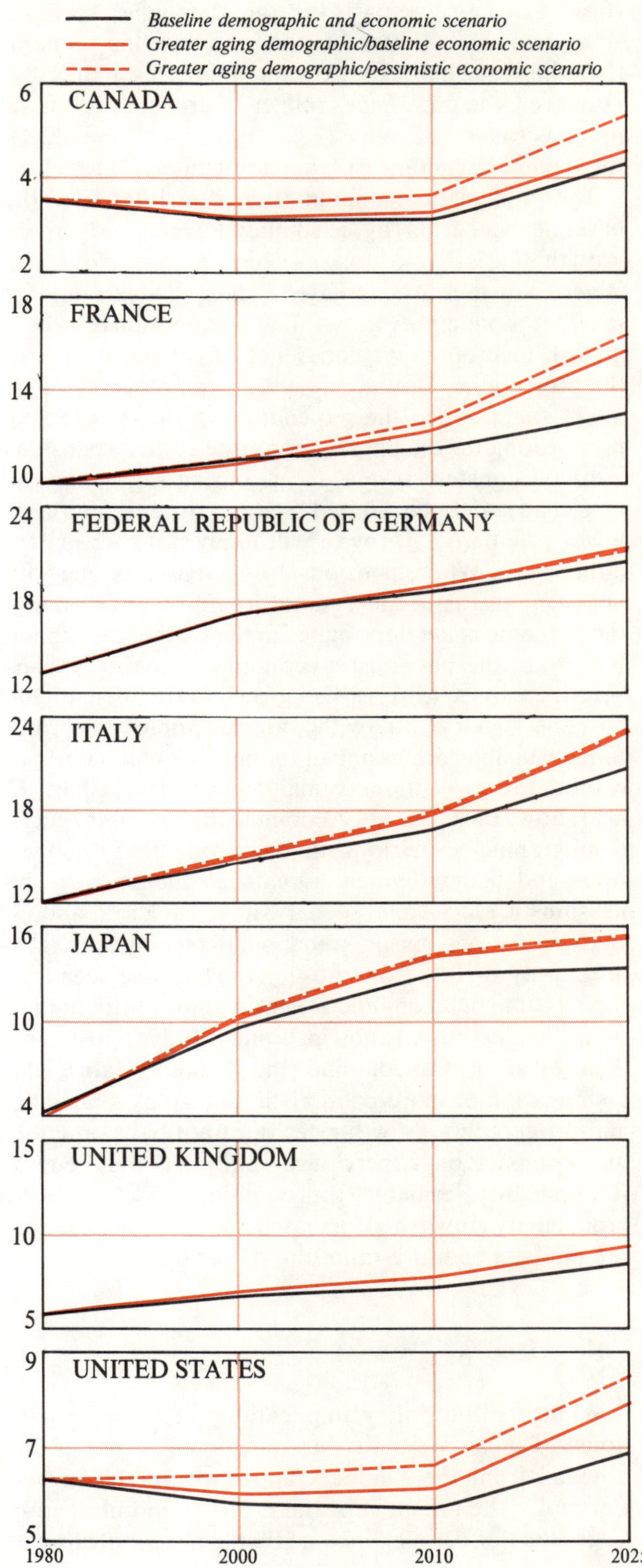

combining the "greater aging" demographic scenario with the baseline economic scenario (see also Table 14). In all countries, final expenditure ratios are higher, although in some countries there is either no difference before 2000 or the expenditure ratios are initially lower (France). In no country is the "greater aging" scenario so much more unfavorable than the baseline scenario that the final expenditure ratio increases markedly. However, the differences reflect 1 percentage point or more as found in France (2.6), Italy (2.4), Japan (2.1), the United Kingdom (1.0), and the United States (1.0).

The pessimistic economic scenarios differ from the baseline scenarios by assuming lower productivity growth and, in most cases, higher unemployment. Where pensions are increased in line with earnings (or in effect productivity growth), an assumption of slower growth in productivity does not affect the results of the projections. However, higher unemployment does affect them, since the expenditure ratio is inversely proportional to the employment rate. Where pensions are held constant in real terms during retirement, as in Canada and the United States, an assumption of lower productivity growth will imply a higher expenditure ratio. Where pensions are increased in line with net earnings, as in the Federal Republic of Germany, the outcome is indeterminate. In the case of the United Kingdom, the pessimistic economic scenario is characterized by a lower GDP growth rate than in the baseline scenario, but by the same unemployment rate. Since pensions are assumed to increase with GDP per capita, the projections remain unaffected. Chart 11 also shows the impact of combining the "greater aging" demographic scenario with the productivity growth rates and unemployment rates that characterize the pessimistic economic scenarios in Tables 2 and 3. Because the pessimistic scenario's unemployment rates differ only slightly from those in the baseline scenario, the pessimistic economic scenario shows little impact on the expenditure ratios in France, Italy, and Japan. And even in Canada and the United States, the combination of more pessimistic unemployment rates and productivity growth rates does not have an enormous impact on expenditure ratios. In the Federal Republic of Germany, the combination of reduced productivity growth and increased unemployment causes the final expenditure ratio to fall slightly.

Policy Issues

What are the policy implications of these projections? The answers to this question are not at all obvious from the numbers appearing in the tables. Certainly, the prospect of the growing and ultimately large share of national income that some countries will have to spend in order to provide the pensions now being promised has been a source of concern. This has been a major issue in the Federal Republic of Germany, Japan, the United Kingdom, and the United States, but it has been less of an issue elsewhere. For example, in Canada, an official report, although recognizing that an aging population would create some additional fiscal pressure, concluded that the high incidence of poverty among pensioners called for an increase in the real level of pensions and that Canada would have the capacity to provide it.[40] And in France, the financial pressures created by population aging are recognized, although recent concern has been with short-term rather than long-term financial imbalances. This concern is reflected in the sort of policy responses being discussed, which revolve around making some attempt to increase the fertility, savings, and participation rates, rather than to reform the pension system. Population aging does not yet seem to be viewed as a pressing issue. In Italy, there is widespread recognition of the need to reform the pension system and a pension reform bill is currently before the Italian Parliament.

Even in the United States, pension reform appears to be less of an issue because a number of measures have already been introduced to counteract the demographic factors that would otherwise force pension expenditure to rise. The projections in Table 6 take account of these measures, which include: the 1977 Social Security Amendment, changing the method of calculation of pensions for those reaching 62 after 1982 so that replacement rates would fall from their 1981 peak until they stabilize in 1990;[41] and the 1983 Social Security Amendment, which legislated an increase in the retirement age from 65 to 67 between 2000 and 2027, introduced changes in early retirement benefits and delayed the retirement credit to be phased in from the beginning of 1986, and subjected to tax half of the pensions of people with high incomes.

Recently, the policy debate has been most active in the Federal Republic of Germany, Japan, and the United Kingdom. Indeed, in the Federal Republic of Germany there has just been a significant change in the pension system, switching the basis of pension increases from gross to net earnings, with the intention that demographically induced increases in social security contribution rates would feed back into smaller

[40] See Canada, Economic Council of Canada (1979). Official projections assume that pensions will increase with earnings; although this is not the current practice, such an assumption provides for an increase in real pension levels. In the baseline economic scenario for Canada, the expenditure ratio in 2025 would rise from 4.3 percent in the current projection to 6.5 percent.

[41] This compensates for a rapid rise in the replacement rate through the mid-1970s because of a flaw in the indexation mechanism introduced in the 1972 Social Security Amendment.

pension increases. This switch has been incorporated into the study's projections. Without it, the projected 2025 expenditure ratio would increase to more than double the 1980 ratio of 13.3 percent of GDP as compared with the 20.5 percent now projected.

In Japan, the ratio of pension expenditure to GDP is projected to grow to the level currently found in the Federal Republic of Germany. But that is more than three times the 1980 level, and would have been substantially higher were it not for the 1985 Pension Reform Act, which reduced the benefit level by up to 37 percent by lowering the replacement rate and eliminating multiple benefits. The reform was motivated by the concern over the long-term viability of the pension scheme: while the large funds now accumulated in the system would have allowed higher pension payments with the current contribution rate to be maintained until the end of this century, the contribution rate would ultimately have had to rise almost fourfold when the accumulated funds ran out. The reform lowered the long-run replacement rate from 83 percent to 68 percent, which effectively freezes the replacement rate at the average level for current new recipients, who have about 32 years of enrollment in the system. Thus, the reform did not have to involve lowering the benefits of current recipients, which helped alleviate controversy over benefit reduction. The reform also unified the Koosei, Kokumin, and Seamen's pension schemes, and pension provisions for spouses have been unified and extended. These measures will rule out the possibility of individuals or households receiving excessive pensions through eligibility under multiple pensions. There is a view that the expenditure ratio anticipated under the revised system is too high, and raising the standard eligibility age from 60 to 65 is under consideration, associated with an extension of the retirement age in general. This could reduce the ratio by about 3 percentage points of GDP.

The United Kingdom has perhaps been taking the most radical look at its pension system in light of the long-term cost implications of SERPS. Its reform strategy has recently been outlined in a policy document.[42] The more expensive elements of SERPS are to be modified: SERPS pensions are to based on lifetime earnings rather than the best 20 years, and calculated on 20 percent of earnings rather than 25 percent. Spouse's rights to inherit SERPS entitlements have been reduced, and greater responsibility has been placed on occupational pension schemes for inflation-proofing guaranteed minimum pensions. Financial incentives are to be introduced for firms setting up occupational schemes and individuals taking out personal pensions. The U.K. Government estimates are that the annual cost of SERPS will be nearly halved by 2033.

The nature of the trade-off currently facing, or which faced, policymakers in each of the seven countries is clear. If projected contribution rates rise too quickly or to unacceptable levels, then future pension expenditure has to be reduced (relative to the projected total), either through a reduction in pension benefits (again relative to their projected level) or an increase in pension age, or a combination of both. The United States has emphasized a phased increase in pension and retirement age while the Federal Republic of Germany, by linking pensions to net earnings rather than gross earnings, will systematically reduce the growth rate of pension expenditure as demographic pressures build up, although contribution rates will remain relatively high. In the United Kingdom, the cost of earnings-related pensions—the principal source of increasing pension expenditure—has been halved, leaving the main structure of SERPS intact. Japan will freeze replacement rates, but this will only partly offset a marked increase in contribution rates. However, because the pension program is immature, there is scope for the contribution rate to increase more than in other countries. Ultimately, France and Italy will respond to demographic pressures, and the Federal Republic of Germany may have to take further measures to control the growth in pension expenditure.

One policy issue that has not yet been mentioned, but has certainly featured in discussions of pension reform, is financing. This paper focuses on expenditure, and the method of financing cannot affect the size of the transfers to the elderly, although it can affect the resources available to meet the pension bill. Most programs are now financed on a pay-as-you-go basis, whereby pensioners are paid out of the current income of the working population. There has been some discussion, especially in the United States, of introducing an element of funding into social security financing—that is, setting aside funds in advance for a pension liability that has to be met. Only Canada and Japan fund part of their social security pension liability, and the trend appears to be toward funding even less.

Both pay-as-you-go and funding have merits, but the proponents of funding highlight its positive impact on saving, capital accumulation, and growth.[43] In fact, research has revealed that the impact of a switch from pay-as-you-go to funding is difficult to determine, although it most likely would lead to more saving.[44] If

[42] United Kingdom, *Reform of Social Security: Programme for Action* (1985).

[43] For a fuller discussion of the alternative methods of social security financing, see International Labor Office (1984).

[44] See Saunders and Klau (1985) for a review of the theoretical and empirical literature dealing with this subject.

this in turn leads to higher growth through increased capital accumulation, then this would make the future pension burden easier to bear. However, a number of issues arise. First, it is not all clear that social security is the most efficient policy instrument available to a government wishing to increase an economy's savings rate. Second, there is no guarantee that a higher government savings rate will lead to higher rates of capital accumulation and growth. And third, the creation of funds large enough to have any significant impact on the future burden of pensions may create problems of monetary management that far outweigh any benefits derived from funding social security.

V Medical Care

In the past two and a half decades, the growth in government expenditure on health and medical care has been explosive, more than doubling as a ratio to GDP in the seven major industrial countries. An increasingly large fraction of the expenditure has been directed toward the elderly population—far greater than its share in the population (Tables 23 and 24). Considering that the aging of industrial country populations will accelerate in coming decades, the issue of rising medical expenditure becomes of particular concern. This chapter focuses on the factors likely to influence the evolution of spending on medical care in the next few decades. Its results will underscore the emphasis placed by most of the seven major industrial countries on the need for containment of medical costs and the implementation of measures to achieve this.

Issues in the Modeling of Long-Term Projections of Medical Expenditure

Among the different types of social expenditure, long-term projections of expenditure on medical care are subject to the greatest uncertainty, reflecting the number and complexity of its determinants. Demographic factors will clearly be important in influencing the growth of medical expenditure. The frequency of illness, its severity, and the complexity of the treatment procedures required are all age-related, dropping sharply after the first year of life and increasing progressively after age 60. This is mirrored by higher medical expenditure for the elderly. For example, in Japan per capita inpatient expenditure is three times greater in the 65–69 age group than in the 15–64 age group; the multiple is more than 5 for the age group 70 and over. In the United Kingdom, an individual aged 75 and over spends, on average, more than twice as much as an individual aged 65–74 and eight times as much as an individual aged 15–64 on all medical services. As the proportion of the elderly increases, the potential demand for medical services should also increase, ceteris paribus (see Table 25).

The expected improvements in life expectancy are not likely to be associated with a significant reduction in morbidity.[45] In fact, the lengthening of the human life span is likely to be associated with chronic illnesses or other disabilities, most of which will require both medical care and other forms of personal care assistance. For example, in the United States, the prevalence of chronic conditions among the elderly is estimated at double that of individuals aged 45–64 and five times that of individuals aged 17–44.[46] It is difficult to predict whether medical advances will limit the impact of the illnesses presently associated with old age and the likely cost of such technologies.

The 1960s and 1970s were periods of significant expansion in the share of the population eligible for public medical insurance programs. Such coverage typically includes inpatient and outpatient care, and in many countries the purchase of pharmaceuticals. Excluding the United States, coverage rates exceed 90 percent of the population for most medical services (Table 26), with typical copayment rates of 90 percent for hospital care. In the United States, coverage was extended to virtually all of the elderly, though more than two thirds of the medical services consumed by the population under age 65 remain privately financed. Thus, with the possible, though unlikely, exception of the United States, expanded population coverage would not be expected to be a factor in explaining the growth of future medical expenditure.

Relative price effects were significant in most countries in explaining the growth of government medical expenditure in the past two decades (OECD (1985)), with the price deflator for medical services rising more rapidly than the GDP deflator in all of the seven major industrial countries except France and Canada (Table 27).[47] The factors underlying these trends are complex, but the institutional characteristics of the systems of medical care delivery have played a major role. On the supply side, the providers of medical care

[45] See Rice and Feldman (1983) and Manton (1982).

[46] United States, U.S. Congress, Senate (1984), p. 5.

[47] One should emphasize that estimating the true price deflator in the medical sector is likely to be subject to considerable error, particularly in light of the rapidity of technological progress in the practice of medicine. There are also likely to be significant differences across countries in the methodology used in estimating this deflator.

have lacked the incentive to provide cost-efficient care because of the fee-for-service nature of reimbursement.

As with other publicly supplied services that are highly labor intensive, limits on the ability to substitute capital for labor may also induce a positive relative price effect. To the extent that medical and paramedical workers are able to maintain their relative income positions vis-à-vis other segments of the labor market for which average labor productivity is rising, this would give rise to a relative price effect, but this may not be sustainable over the longer term particularly in those countries where physicians' salaries are relatively high. Government policy plays a critical role in this regard. Even in countries where the government is not the direct employer of most medical and paramedical workers, its role as a third party financing agent is so important that it can exert a dampening impact on the market power of the medical profession and of the industries supplying medical equipment, supplies, and drugs. Such government actions have become increasingly more common in almost all of the seven major industrial countries.

The average growth in real benefits has been the dominant factor underlying the growth in real expenditure on medical care in the past two decades. Estimates by the OECD suggest that average real benefits rose by 6.5 percent a year between 1960 and 1975 and by almost 3 percent annually between 1975 and 1981 for the seven major industrial countries as a whole (Table 27). This is in contrast to a relative price effect of about 1 percent annually and to demographic and coverage effects of significantly less than 1 percent annually over the whole period. In using the OECD historical results to determine appropriate assumptions for this study's projections, it should be noted that, under the OECD methodology, the statistics on the past growth in average real benefits in the medical care sector are likely to be overstated to the extent that they are inclusive of what this present study would categorize as demographic effects. Specifically, in the OECD study, the growth in average real benefits in the medical sector is calculated as a residual (e.g., net of the effect of demographic factors, the expansion in client coverage, and relative price effects). Since their demographic effects do not take account of the change in the age structure that occurred between 1960 and 1981 (but rather only the change in the size of the total population), it is likely that some of the imputed growth in average real benefits simply reflects the effect of a shift toward the elderly in the age composition of the recipients and the higher per capita medical expenses of the elderly. Evidence on the shift in the age composition and on the growth of average real benefits between 1960 and 1980 is provided in Table 28.

When breaking down the factors that are likely to determine the growth of real expenditure per capita (net of coverage, demographic, and relative price effects), the complexity of the underlying relationships becomes apparent. Factors involving the degree of autonomy and discretion of the consumer, the medical practitioner, and the medical institutions in their choice of the quantity and quality of care to be provided are at the heart of the process. These factors include the extent to which financial constraints impinge on the decision-making process and influence the incentive to economize in the choice of care. This incentive is critically shaped by the nature of the medical insurance system prevailing in a country. Where open-ended third party financing systems operate, there may be little incentive for the medical practitioner to limit the services provided or to provide cost-efficient care.[48] Historically, the high level and indeed the increasing share of payments by third party insurers (whether government or private) has insulated patients from the cost of medical services. Where the practitioners have the effective market power to set the cost of services, this may further stimulate a rise in costs. In situations where government-imposed budget constraints determine the available resources to a hospital or practitioner, as in the United Kingdom, it would be expected that the quantity and quality of services provided for a given episode of illness would be significantly different.

Another factor likely to influence average benefits is the development of medical technology. Many of the new medical techniques allow for treatments thought infeasible until recently. They are also quite costly. Technological progress in the medical sector has tended to focus more on improving the quality and scope of medical care than providing existing services in a less costly fashion. The demand for more sophisticated technology is likely to be bolstered by expectations on the demand side as real income levels rise, with the negative effects of higher prices on consumer expectations being dampened to the extent of limited patient-copayment formulas. On the other hand, in most countries a significant gap is still evident between the development of such medical techniques and their effective availability to the average patient in need of them.

In effect, national statistics on government medical expenditure per capita (i.e., average benefits) by age group in a given period, and their growth over time, are a reflection of the cumulative impact of various

[48] It is tempting to characterize this as a U.S. phenomenon. It is not. For example, a recent expert on the French medical system in the late 1970s noted that "medical care became increasingly technically oriented and the hospital-based physicians had neither utility criteria nor financial incentives to seek the least costly procedures in diagnosis or treatment" (Laurois, cited in Godt (1985), p. 160).

economic, institutional, and technological factors. Historically, this impact has resulted in a dramatic growth in average benefits far exceeding the rate of growth of productivity in the countries in this study. Equally clear, the factors inducing the growth in benefits are not wholly exogenous and can be influenced by public policy measures. Indeed, the government plays a very direct role in the process through its role as a third party financing agent. Even where the government's role is smaller (as in the United States), private third party financing is encouraged by government tax subsidies. Governments are now increasingly concerned about the cost of medical care and are moving to implement policies to achieve some degree of control (see the section on Policy Issues below). This being said, it is difficult to judge the likely degree of success of such policies.

In view of these many uncertainties, the projection model used in this study was deliberately kept simple. Country-specific estimates of average expenditure for medical care per capita in 1980,[49] disaggregated by age group and by type of medical service (inpatient, outpatient, drugs), were obtained. Several estimates were then made as to the possible growth of real expenditure per capita. In effect, such growth rates will reflect the *joint* effect of any further expansion (or reduction) in coverage, any relative price effect, and any growth in real benefits and intensity of demand arising from the multiplicity of factors mentioned above. Such a growth rate will be denoted as the growth of the "medical costs" variable. One assumption would limit the growth in real medical costs per capita to the growth in productivity, with the rate of increase assumed to be equal across the different types of medical service. This assumption is effectively equivalent to evaluating the pure demographic effect on the ratio of medical expenditure to GDP, holding productivity constant at 1980 levels.[50]

By historical standards, this assumption would represent a significant moderation in the growth of medical expenditure per capita (Table 7), particularly in France, Japan, and the United States, where the combined growth rate of average benefits and the relative price effect has been more than double that of both the historical growth in productivity during the period 1974–84 and the assumed future productivity growth used in these projections. For the remaining countries, limiting the growth in the medical costs variable to the rate of growth of productivity would represent a significant slowdown from recent historical experience.

A scenario more closely corresponding with historical experience on medical costs, but also compatible with assumptions made by country sources, would assume rates of growth in the medical costs variable that exceed the rate of productivity growth by 0.3–0.9 percentage points annually. With the exception of Canada, growth rates for this cost variable are assumed to be less than those experienced during the period 1975–81. The model does not attempt to impose expenditure ceilings per se, so that specific government policies that set ceilings on overall expenditure (such

[49] In most cases, such estimates were directly available from country sources. In other cases (notably France, Italy, and Japan), estimates were available on the age-specific intensity of the use of particular types of medical services. Based on the average cost of a given medical service, an estimate could then indirectly be made for the average expenditure on that type of service, assuming that the average cost per case of individuals is invariant across age groups (see Table 25). In the countries for which data are available, the latter assumption does not appear to be far out of line.

[50] In calculating the pure demographic effect, output would be adjusted only to take account of demographically induced changes in the size of the labor force and the unemployment rate. In the United States, economic effects on the labor force participation rate are also included in the various scenarios.

Table 7. Cost and Productivity Factors Assumed in the Medical Sector Projection Model and Historical Statistics

(In annual percentages)

Country	Assumed Growth in: Medical costs variable	Assumed Growth in: Productivity	Productivity Growth	Historical Statistics: Sum of relative price effect and average real benefit growth rate	
	1980–2025		1974–84	1960–75	1975–81
Canada	2.0	1.5	0.5	6.9	1.8
France	2.5	2.0	2.2	8.6	4.9
Germany, Fed. Rep. of	2.5	2.0	2.4	7.4	2.8
Italy	2.5	2.2	1.1	7.2	3.2
Japan	3.5	3.0	2.6	15.1	6.7
United Kingdom	2.0	1.4	1.6	4.9	2.2
United States	2.5	1.6	0.3	5.1	4.7

Sources: OECD, *Social Expenditure: 1960–1990, Problems of Growth and Control* (1985); OECD, *Economic Outlook*, various issues; and Fund staff estimates.

as the cash-limits approach to budgeting in the United Kingdom) would not be directly reflected.[51] Other cross-country differences in policy and their effects on costs are subsumed within the assumption on the growth rate of the medical costs variable.

The model takes 1980 as the base year and does not take account of changes in the ratio of medical expenditure to GDP between 1980 and the present. To the extent that actual costs have risen faster than assumed here (e.g., in Canada and the United States), the projected expenditure ratio would be understated unless medical costs could be brought back to the trend implied by these projections.

Finally, these projections relate only to the growth in personal medical care outlays. Additional public expenditure on capital investment in medical care, medical research and education, and medical administration additionally account for up to 1 percent of GDP in those countries for which data are readily available (i.e., Canada, Italy, and the United States). For the purpose of projections of total social expenditure, such expenditures are assumed to remain constant as a percentage of GDP (and are included in the projections of medical expenditure indicated in Table 14).[52]

Table 8. Real Government Expenditure on Medical Care, 1980–2025[1]

(Index: 1980 = 100)

Country	1980	2000	2010	2025
	Baseline demographic scenario			
Canada	100	128	140	174
France	100	117	125	130
Germany, Fed. Rep. of	100	104	107	103
Italy	100	113	117	121
Japan	100	130	140	147
United Kingdom	100	105	105	115
United States	100	130	144	180
	"Greater aging" demographic scenario			
Canada	100	130	142	174
France	100	120	129	149
Germany, Fed. Rep. of	100	103	105	100
Italy	100	114	118	123
Japan	100	139	150	153
United Kingdom	100	106	108	119
United States	100	132	148	188

Source: Fund staff estimates.

[1] Excluding expenditure on medical research and education, administration, and capital investment in the medical sector; assumes no increase in real expenditure per capita by age group over 1980 levels.

Medical Expenditure Projections, 1980–2025

Table 8 presents, in index form, the effects of demographic developments on the absolute level of medical care expenditure, assuming no increase in real expenditure per recipient in any age group or in coverage (i.e., simply the effect on outlays of the change in size and structure of the population). There is a sharp divergence in growth across countries, ranging from only a modest increase in the Federal Republic of Germany, Italy, and the United Kingdom to a substantial increase in Canada, Japan, and the United States. The development of real spending reflects two factors: changes in the age structure and the absolute size of the population.

Thus, while a more aging population tends to have more rapidly growing expenditure, if other things remain constant, this can be offset by the scale factor. The Federal Republic of Germany's population ages much faster than that of France, Italy, and the United Kingdom, but it shows a smaller expenditure growth because of a declining population size. Medical expenditure in France will grow much faster than in the United Kingdom, despite slower aging and a lower initial expenditure share on the elderly, because of faster growth in the population. It is also interesting to compare Canada and the United States. Canada's population is aging more rapidly and will have a slightly faster growth in its total population, yet in the United States expenditure on medical care will grow somewhat more rapidly. The reason lies in the much higher share of government expenditure on medical care that is allocated to the elderly in the United States (Table 23).

Neither scenario would be particularly worrisome for any country if demographic factors alone were the only influence on the growth of real medical expenditure. Such a growth in expenditure would be small in comparison to the growth in total output, so that the ratio of medical expenditure to GDP would drop to 70 percent of its present value by the year 2000 and would be even lower in subsequent years. This scenario would be extremely unlikely, given the historical evidence that suggests that medical costs per capita will continue to rise in real terms.

Chart 12 illustrates the effects of the assumption that real medical costs per capita rise at the same rate as productivity. This assumption is equivalent to estimating the effects of demographics on the ratio of government expenditure on medical care to GDP, holding output per worker constant at 1980 levels (and adjusting the size of the labor force for demographic

[51] However, the growth in the medical costs variable assumed for the United Kingdom does take account of historical cost control efforts.

[52] Such expenditures do not represent a significant share of total medical care expenditure and are likely to be influenced by different underlying pressures.

Chart 12. Government Medical Care as a Percentage of GDP, 1980–2025

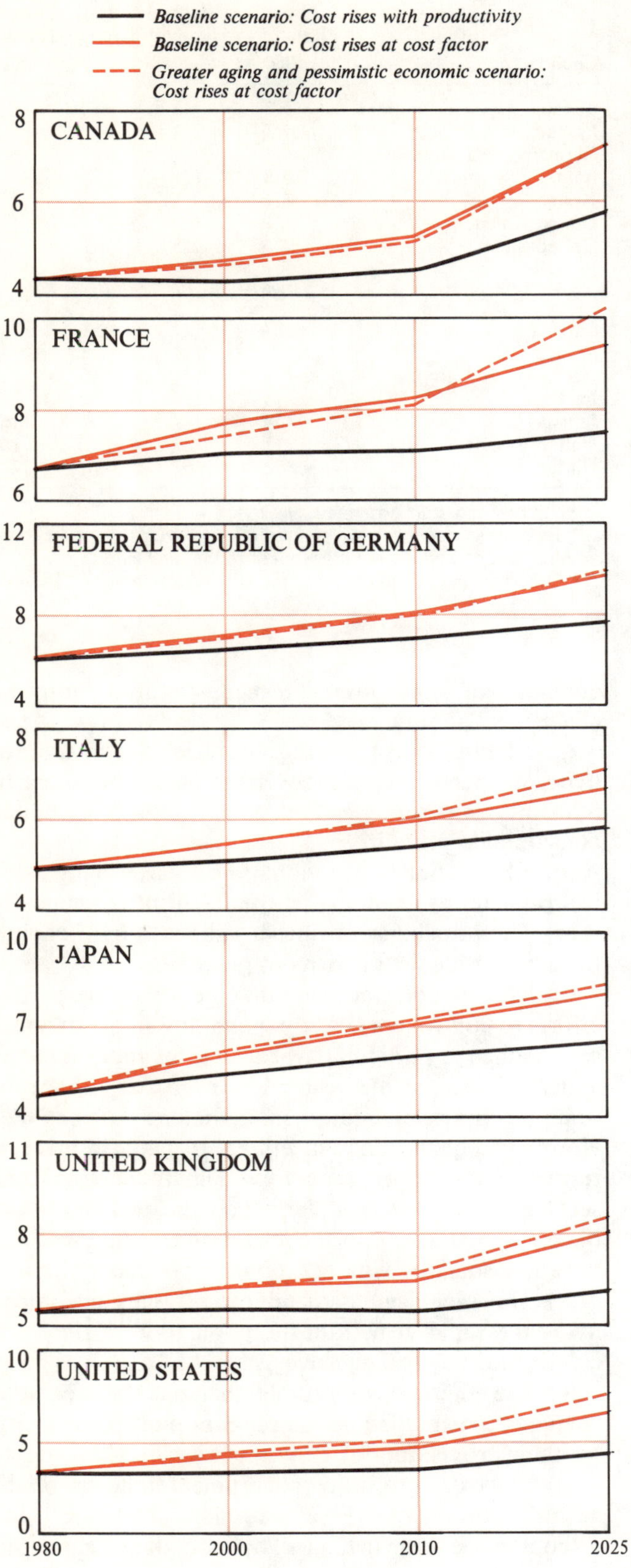

and unemployment trends). It significantly modifies the picture implied in Table 8, particularly for Canada, the Federal Republic of Germany, and the United States. The rapid growth of total expenditure in Canada and the United States is accompanied by significant population growth. Once allowance is made for the increased labor force, the expenditure ratio is seen to grow substantially less. In the Federal Republic of Germany, on the other hand, the low growth in real expenditure in Table 8 is due to a declining population size. When the declining labor force is taken into account, the burden of the pure demographic effect is as large as in Canada or in the United States. In four countries (Canada, the Federal Republic of Germany, Japan, and the United States), the ratio of government medical expenditure to GDP rises by 26–34 percent over the 45-year period—the equivalent of approximately 1.6 percent of GDP in the first three countries and 1 percent of GDP in the United States. For the three other countries, lower growth rates are projected, with the ratio of medical expenditure to GDP rising by 0.7–0.9 percentage points by 2025.

A more realistic scenario would assume average medical costs rising more rapidly than productivity, as indicated in Table 7. This results in a substantial increase in the ratio of medical expenditure to GDP over the whole period (Chart 12). By the year 2000, the ratio will increase by approximately 0.4–1.2 percentage points of GDP, rising particularly rapidly in France, the Federal Republic of Germany, and Japan. Between 2000 and 2010, further increases in the ratio would occur, again raising it by approximately 0.4–1.0 percentage points of GDP. The United Kingdom is an exception in this regard, with the medical expenditure ratio rising only slightly.[53] The most dramatic increase in the expenditure ratio would be observed between 2010 and 2025, particularly in Canada and the United States, but also to a significant extent in the Federal Republic of Germany, Italy, Japan, and the United Kingdom. By the year 2025, government medical expenditure will have almost doubled as a ratio of GDP in the United States and will be approximately 60–70 percent higher in Canada, the Federal Republic of Germany, Italy, and Japan, relative to 1980.

It is important to stress that approximately two thirds of the prospective increase in the medical expenditure ratio to GDP derives from the difference between the growth in the medical costs variable and the rate of productivity growth in the economy. A growth of 0.5 percent a year relative to productivity adds about 25 percentage points to the absolute level

[53] This result reflects past behavior and does not fully take account of the effects of the cash-limits approach to the budgeting of medical expenditure in the United Kingdom.

of expenditure by the end of the 45-year period. Thus, the assumed rate of growth of costs relative to productivity growth has great potential to exacerbate or alleviate the demographic effect.[54]

Adoption of more pessimistic economic assumptions and the "greater aging" scenario leads to a higher medical expenditure ratio, but with the exception of France, not dramatically so. Through the year 2010, the ratio is no more than 0.3 percentage points of GDP higher in any of the countries than in the baseline scenario. However, between 2010 and 2025, the assumption of "greater aging" in the population leads to a significantly greater increase in the expenditure ratio (relative to the baseline scenario) in France and the United States, rising in these countries by a further 1.3 and 1.0 percentage points of GDP, respectively. Relative to 1980, the impact of aging on medical expenditure is greatest in Japan and the United States; in the case of the United States, the higher share of medical care expenditure on the elderly offsets its slower aging.

The importance of immediate efforts to contain costs is illustrated in Table 9. The column for 1980 indicates the ratio of medical expenditure to GDP in 2025 *if, as of 1980*, the medical costs variable were to rise no faster than productivity. The remaining columns indicate the expenditure ratios that would prevail in 2025 if costs were to rise at the assumed cost factor of Table 7 through 2000, 2010, and 2025, respectively.

Delay of such efforts to contain costs to the year 2000 would add approximately 0.7 percentage points of GDP in medical care expenditure, using the historically conservative cost factors indicated in Table 7; delay to the year 2010 would add 1.2–1.5 percentage points of GDP. This assumption of delay highlights the importance of the efforts for cost containment currently underway in these countries—and which are likely to be emphasized even more as the demographic situation changes.

Table 9. Effect of Delaying Medical Cost Control Efforts: Medical Expenditure in 2025 as a Ratio to GDP[1]

Country	Growth in Medical Costs Held to Rate of Productivity Growth as of:[2] 1980	2000	2010	2025
Canada	5.5	6.3	6.7	7.2
France	7.5	8.3	8.7	9.4
Germany, Fed. Rep. of	7.7	8.4	8.9	9.7
Italy	5.8	6.1	6.4	6.7
Japan	6.4	7.1	7.5	8.1
United Kingdom	6.1	6.9	7.3	8.0
United States	4.4	5.5	5.9	6.6
	(Relative to 1980 ratio to GDP)			
Canada	127	144	153	166
France	112	124	130	140
Germany, Fed. Rep. of	126	137	145	159
Italy	118	125	130	137
Japan	134	149	157	169
United Kingdom	112	127	133	146
United States	132	167	178	200

Source: Fund staff estimates.
[1] Excluding expenditure on medical research and education, administration, and capital investment in the medical sector.
[2] Otherwise, assumed to rise at the cost factor shown in Table 7.

Policy Issues

Several issues are likely to appear on the agenda for health and medical care policy in the foreseeable future and will have important consequences for the evolution of expenditure on medical care. These include:

(a) Elimination of existing inefficiencies in the delivery of specific medical services. This is particularly relevant in a period when budgetary outlays are under considerable pressure.

(b) Elimination of questionable excesses in the medical procedures used for the treatment of cases.

(c) The possibility of further substitution of capital for labor in medical treatment practices.

(d) The implicit trade-offs that inevitably arise from efforts to control costs and expenditure in the medical care industry, particularly at a time of rapid technological change in medical science. In part, this is a trade-off between equity and efficiency objectives. However, equally difficult ethical issues also arise in regard to the appropriate treatment technology and services for the very elderly and the terminally ill, raising questions as to the value of the marginal net benefit associated with additional increments of care.

(e) The increased demand for services accompanying the rapid growth in the population of the very elderly (i.e., age 80 and over).

(f) The emerging structural imbalances between the changing demand for health services and the capacity for their provision.

(g) The extent to which government policies should be used to encourage a healthier "life-style" (or discourage adverse behavior) by individuals, given the

[54] For reference, if average medical expenditure per capita grew at the rate actually experienced during 1975–81, and assuming the prospective productivity growth rates indicated in Table 7, the change in the ratio of government medical expenditure to GDP would be dramatic in some countries, as indicated below:

	1980	2025		1980	2025
Canada	4.4	6.4	Japan	4.8	31.5
France	6.7	26.0	United Kingdom	5.5	8.7
Germany, Fed. Rep. of	6.1	10.9	United States	3.3	16.9
Italy	4.9	9.0			

evidence that many medical problems are behavioral in origin.

(h) The effect of new diseases on the average cost of providing medical care.

Most countries in this study have been preoccupied in recent years with the problem of controlling the growth of government expenditure on medical care, and cost containment is likely to continue to be a major priority in the foreseeable future. In part, this has taken the form of efforts to improve the efficiency with which services are provided—to eliminate excess capacity, to offset imperfections or excessive power in the market through which medical services and supplies are provided, and to eliminate the degree to which almost 100 percent third party copayment rates have led to excessive demand for medical care by patients and excessive supply of services by physicians and hospitals. Other policies have attempted to shift a greater share of the cost burden to the insured population and to increase their cost consciousness.

A brief and by no means comprehensive survey will suffice to illustrate the types of policies emphasized in some of the countries. Changes in reimbursement procedures to hospitals and physicians have been introduced in several countries as a means of precluding an excessive pass-through of charges to medical insurance systems.[55] Such changes have been associated with efforts to limit the increase in the reimbursement rate over time. The introduction by the United States in 1983 of a prospective payment system for inpatient care is one example.[56] In Italy, changes have been made in the reimbursement procedure for general practitioners. In Japan, actions have been taken to reduce "excessive treatment" through closer monitoring of claims and periodic revisions to the reimbursement price to reflect the actual cost of medicine and medical treatment.

In the Federal Republic of Germany, since the mid-1970s, the government has followed a policy aimed at containing expenditure growth, partly through legislative changes but also through negotiations with physicians' associations, hospitals, and representatives of health insurance companies and the pharmaceutical industry. These actions have led to some restraint in the volume of services provided and to modifications in the tariff structure of medical services. In late 1984, the German Government also attempted to provide greater profit incentives to hospitals as a means of containing costs.

In Canada, physician profiles are constructed from claims data in order to identify physicians whose billing patterns deviate sharply from the average. Those with excessive billing are subject to the possibility of sanctions. In addition, global caps are imposed on total reimbursements for physicians (see United States, U.S. Congress, Congressional Budget Office (1986)).

In France, policies were introduced in 1980 to limit physicians' fees through a uniform fee schedule mechanism and in 1984 to set an annual ceiling for hospital expenditures, forcing hospitals to live within fixed means (Godt (1985) and Laurois (1984)). This latter policy has already led to some self-restraint by hospitals (as manifested by a decline in the average length of stay). Direct authority was also given to the Ministry of Health to phase out excess bed capacity in government hospitals. Finally, in France, the Federal Republic of Germany, and the United States, reimbursement rates have not been allowed to capture the full effects of inflation.

These changes directly affect the incentive system facing suppliers of medical care and hopefully lead to more cost-effective procedures. Whether these changes will actually reduce overall costs is not yet clear.[57] For example, in the United States, the changes in the reimbursement system have led to a reduction in the average length of stay in hospitals. It is not yet clear whether this has been offset by increased admissions, a shifting of care to an outpatient basis (where a prospective payment system has not yet been introduced), or by a tendency to classify patients according to more expensive diagnostic categories.

Governments have also attempted to increase the share of costs borne by the individual, both as a means of increasing the share of financing by the private sector and also as a means of discouraging wasteful consumption of medical services. In Japan, for individuals under age 70, the enrollee's copayment rate was recently increased under the Health Care Act from 0 to 10 percent (subject to certain major medical provisions); for individuals over age 70, inpatient and outpatient care, which was previously free, is now subject to a nominal charge. Recent evidence suggests that total medical payments to insurees in the three months since implementation were 10 percent below the level of the previous year (the first decline in the monthly data since 1971).[58] In Italy, patients are now required to pay some part of the cost of drugs. In the United States, legislative efforts are underway to

[55] For an interesting discussion of recent policies to contain reimbursements to physicians in Canada, the Federal Republic of Germany, and the United States, see United States, U.S. Congress, Congressional Budget Office (1986).

[56] See United States, Council of Economic Advisers (1985).

[57] For a fuller discussion of alternative approaches to the prospective payment system, see United States, Council of Economic Advisers (1985), pp. 149–50.

[58] "Enrollee Health Costs Down 10 Percent." See *Yomiuri Shimbun* (1985).

increase both the copayment rate and the contribution rate by pensioners with respect to Medicare. In France, a minimum day-rate payment imposed in 1984 created an incentive for patients to reduce hospital stays (Godt (1985), p. 163).

Though the approaches described above may discourage wasteful consumption, particularly of ambulatory care and drugs, significant cost-sharing will prove more difficult in situations where expensive hospitalization is required, thus defeating the purpose of insurance. Also, increased cost-sharing for some services can lead to substitution in demand for other services for which the individual's copayment rates are lower.

Another issue relates to whether individuals should bear higher copayment rates according to their life-style or habits (e.g., smoking, excessive drinking, taking drugs, etc., which increase the risk of illness). In effect, should individuals not be encouraged to lead healthier life-styles, rather than taxed to support the more medically costly life-styles of others?

Finally, it should be noted that some governments have been moving toward an overall ceiling on government medical expenditure. Such a ceiling exists already in the United Kingdom, whereby approximately 80 percent of expenditures on medical care are "cash-limited" and subject to extensive efforts to minimize the limits of expenditure totals. This ceiling brought about a sharp slowdown in the rate of increase of public expenditure on health and medical care from an average annual rate of about 5 percent between 1960 and 1975 to about 2 percent during the period 1975–81. The Canadian federal authorities replaced an essentially open-ended cost-sharing formula for the provinces with a fixed revenue-sharing formula, thus pressuring the regional authorities to rationalize their delivery systems, modify copayment rates, and limit physicians' earnings. In Italy, the "regionalization" of hospitals under the new National Health System represented an attempt to impose some overall limits on the growth in medical expenditure, though this has not been very successful to date.[59]

Cash limits will succeed only if efficiency gains prevent reductions in service. The authorities of the United Kingdom recognize that the demographic pressures of an aging population will be associated with increased demand for medical services and that technological advances are likely to lead to a net increase in costs. These developments will not necessarily be reflected in an increase in cash-limited health programs. In effect, cash limits provide an incentive constantly to search for improvements in efficiency—otherwise new services can only be introduced at the cost of cutting back existing services.

Ultimately, however, the difficult issue becomes one of controlling costs without compromising other policy objectives, particularly with respect to the quality of care provided. Rapidly changing technology further complicates this trade-off. While technological change in medical science can lighten the trade-off, allowing improved quality of care to be purchased less expensively, many new developments portend the capacity, albeit expensive, to improve substantially the prospects for surviving previously fatal illnesses. Will it be necessary to ration the more expensive technologies, and if so, what criteria will be applied? How does one judge the marginal benefits of additional treatment? Should the cost of repair or transplant of critical human organs be covered by health insurance programs and, if so, how should the costs be distributed among participants?

These issues become particularly complex for the very elderly and raise difficult ethical issues. In the United States, more than a quarter of total Medicare spending arose from the treatment of enrollees in the last year of their life, even though such enrollees constituted only 5 percent of the enrolled population.[60] How much of such expenditure was of "lifesaving" value? Could there have been a shift of care from more expensive hospitals to less expensive hospices?[61] At what point does one cease to pursue intensive medical treatment of the hopelessly ill or of those who are senile? Conversely, should mentally competent patients have the right to refuse life-sustaining medical treatment?

Another issue that will become increasingly relevant, and fraught with cost implications, is long-term chronic care for the very elderly. It was noted in Chapter III that the very elderly (i.e., individuals 80 and over) are the most rapidly growing segment of the population. The relatively greater need for medical expenditure for this group, under the *existing* system of coverage and benefits, is covered in the above projections (albeit imperfectly, for lack of disaggregated data). However, this group will have additional needs that are only partially covered under the present social insurance systems of most countries.[62] The prevalence of chronic illness conditions, serious activity limitations, and the

[59] Mapelli (1984) provides a discussion of the National Health System reform.

[60] See United States, Council of Economic Advisers (1985).

[61] The impact on costs of proposals to fund hospice care under government medical insurance programs is uncertain. Will the effects of substitution of a less expensive form of care be offset by the possibility of a sharp increase in demand for this service from families and individuals that previously had not been receiving benefits for this type of care?

[62] For a detailed study of the arrangements for caring for the very elderly in the industrial countries, see United States, U.S. Congress, Senate (1984).

need for assistance in the activities of daily living is dramatically greater for this age group.

> In the U.S., persons age 65 and older are almost five times more likely to suffer activity limitations than persons under 65 years, and persons age 85 and older are twice as likely to suffer activity limitations as persons aged 65 to 74. Persons over 75 are over 20 times more likely to need personal care assistance in at least one activity of daily living (such as bathing, dressing, eating, and toileting) than are persons under age 65. Thus, in addition to a growing need for acute care, an aging population will also be accompanied by a growing need for long-term and maintenance care, including a vast array of social services as well as personal care.[63]

Such conditions as Alzheimer's disease, arthritis, limiting heart conditions, hypertension, osteoporosis (bone disease), incontinence, hearing and vision failure, and depression become increasingly common in the older age groups. More importantly, with age, an individual is more likely to experience more than one of the above conditions.

Should there be an expansion in the coverage of social insurance to provide more comprehensive coverage for alternatives to hospital care for the very aged (e.g., in nursing homes, old age homes, congregate and sheltered housing, home health care, homemaker care, adult day care, respite care)? Present social insurance for nursing homes or other alternatives is limited in most countries. In fact, much of the heavy (or often inappropriate) utilization of high-cost, acute-care hospital capacity for the treatment of the chronically ill elderly population derives from the higher certainty of coverage of the cost of hospitalization under most government medical insurance schemes. As with hospice benefits, it is uncertain whether expanded insurance coverage of nursing home facilities would reduce the cost to the insurance schemes of such care, as the expanded coverage might well offset whatever substitution effect arises from a shift out of acute-care and psychiatric hospitals.

[63] United States, U.S. Congress, Senate (1984), p. 5.

With the shift in the age structure of the population, an associated change will take place in the underlying structure of demand for services, creating imbalances between available physical capacity and professional manpower resources and the structure of demand. This change will undoubtedly create short-term transitional adjustment difficulties. For example, the share of government expenditure on medical care consumed by the age group 65 and over will substantially increase. In the Federal Republic of Germany, Italy, and the United Kingdom, it will increase by 7–9 percentage points between 1980 and 2025; in Canada, Japan, and the United States, the increase will be even more dramatic (Table 10). This increased share will be reflected in a change in the demand for particular services, with obviously increased needs for nursing home facilities and for professionals and paraprofessionals trained in geriatric care. An associated problem will be the need to "retool" plants and retrain professionals in specialities less in demand.

Table 10. Percentage of Government Medical Care Expenditure on the Elderly Population, as Projected in the Baseline Scenarios, 1980–2025[1]

Country	1980	2000	2010	2025
Canada	33.3	38.0	40.9	53.1
France	...	...	...	...
Germany, Fed. Rep. of[2]	33.1	33.6	39.0	42.6
Italy	31.8	36.2	37.4	40.6
Japan	27.4	37.7	43.8	48.3
United Kingdom	42.1	44.1	44.3	49.4
United States	50.0	54.4	55.6	64.6

Source: Fund staff estimates.
[1] Costs rise as assumed in Table 7.
[2] Over age 60.

VI Education

As much as for any other social program, the demand for education is influenced vitally by demographic factors. After a long period of expansion, the education system of most of the countries has entered or is about to enter a period of decline in the number of students as a consequence of low fertility rates. In principle, this decline should yield savings in expenditure to offset some of the increased pension and health costs associated with the aging of the population. This chapter estimates the magnitude of such possible savings, but argues that the potential savings implied by projected demographic developments may not be fully realized because of the specific cost structures and structural rigidities of the education systems in some countries.

The Structure of the Education Sector

At first glance, the structure of the education systems of all seven major industrial countries appears to be similar: 12–13 years of schooling are offered, of which 8–10 are compulsory. In the past two decades, there has also been a tendency to lengthen the years of compulsory schooling, either to unify different school systems or to alleviate the pressure of the growing population on the labor market. Differences across countries are primarily reflected in the number of years associated with different levels of schooling (Table 29). Nevertheless, there are common features other than the number of years of schooling offered. Public schools predominate, and the government exerts an important supervisory role over the curriculum and the examination system in private institutions. Private sector activities in regard to education play a subordinate role within the overall system and have a sizable share, if at all, only at the preprimary and postsecondary or tertiary levels (primarily in Japan and the United States). Public policies on education in all countries, with the exception of France, are the concern of provincial or state governments and not of the central government. Furthermore, teachers usually have lifetime tenure in the public sector, and in a number of countries teachers' benefits have been adjusted over time to the level received by other civil servants. The special employment status of teachers may introduce downward rigidities that may constrain employment policy options in the education sector in the face of declining enrollment.

Past Developments

Expenditure on education grew rapidly as a percentage of GDP in all countries under study between 1960 and 1975, with the expenditure ratio increasing by more than 50 percent, to 5 percent of GDP, by 1975 in most countries. The growth was especially pronounced in Canada, with the ratio of education expenditure to GDP reaching 8 percent. After 1975, education expenditure declined somewhat in most countries except for Italy and Japan, where education expenditure expanded as a percentage of GDP throughout the 1970s.

Two main factors appear responsible for past developments. First, a substantial increase in enrollments occurred (Table 30), reflecting the movement of the postwar "baby boom" generation into school age, compulsory schooling, and a rising demand for noncompulsory higher education (Table 31). Attendance at preprimary education facilities increased continuously in most countries between 1950 and 1980, primarily as a response to the higher labor force participation rates of women. Second, the cost per student increased during the 1970s. This was principally the result of increasing teacher-pupil ratios, as demographic pressures abated, but also was influenced by increases in teachers' salaries. Several aspects of these developments are worth noting.

The expansion of the education system in the 1960s and early 1970s took place at a time of generous public-spending policies. Education was perceived as a vehicle for advancement and opportunity for the poor. Education was also considered to be a key factor in sustaining and promoting steady economic growth. With the rapidly increasing size of the student age group, governments accommodated the increased demand for education by expanding educational facilities and increasing the teaching staff. Expenditure on education began to decline only after 1975, coinciding with the decline of the total school population in all countries except Japan and with a more restrictive fiscal policy stance. Although there was a decline in overall enrollment by 1975, different school levels were affected at different times by the movement of the postwar "baby boom" generation through the education system.

The expansion of the education system was reflected in increased investment during the 1960s and early 1970s, when more facilities were provided. This expansion was paralleled by an increase in the number of teaching staff. Recurrent education expenditure continued to grow even when investment declined sharply. Owing to a lack of teachers in the 1950s and 1960s, teacher remuneration improved substantially over time to attract more students to this profession. Consequently, over the last 30 years, the teacher-pupil ratio increased markedly at the primary level. Between 1950 and 1975 the improvement in this ratio at the primary level was due to the number of staff increasing faster than the number of students, while thereafter the ratio improved further because of the decline in the number of students.

The employment of teachers was not adjusted to the lower number of students, since in most countries teachers have lifetime tenure and thus cannot be readily laid off. Most governments, except for the United States, used the opportunity of the abating demographic pressure to deliberately allow for an improvement in the teacher-pupil ratio as a way of strengthening the quality of the educational system. At the secondary level, an overall improvement in the teacher-pupil ratio was not recorded, as increases in the number of staff could barely keep pace with the growing number of students in the 1970s. However, because of the special status of teachers, declining enrollment at the secondary level in the 1980s is likely to result in an improvement of the teacher-pupil ratio at this level as well.

Table 11. Overall School Enrollments, 1980–2025

(Index: 1980 = 100)

Country	1980	2000	2010	2025
		Baseline scenarios		
Canada	100	99	97	100
France	100	101	99	103
Germany, Fed. Rep. of	100	84	74	66
Italy	100	82	84	77
Japan	100	81	88	86
United Kingdom	100	86	86	85
United States	100	101	99	103
		"Greater aging" scenarios		
Canada	100	99	97	99
France	100	97	94	92
Germany, Fed. Rep. of	100	76	64	52
Italy	100	78	74	64
Japan	100	80	81	68
United Kingdom	100	85	80	73
United States	100	94	85	77

Source: Fund staff estimates.

Education Expenditure Projections, 1980–2025

The projections of the baseline demographic scenario suggest that only Canada, France, and the United States will be able to maintain the present size of their school populations over the next 45 years (Table 11). All other countries will experience a sharp reduction in enrollments between 1980 and 2025. In the next 20 years, the lowest number of students will be recorded in the Federal Republic of Germany and Italy (by 1990) and in the United Kingdom (by 1995). Thereafter, overall enrollment will increase only moderately and reach local peaks in all countries except Japan between 2000 and 2005. Japan will experience this peak somewhat later. From then on a continuous decline in enrollments will take place in the Federal Republic of Germany, Italy, Japan, and the United Kingdom until the end of the projection period. By 2025, the school population in the Federal Republic of Germany will be almost 35 percent lower than in 1980, in Italy 24 percent lower, and in Japan and the United Kingdom 15 percent lower. These movements reflect a combination of diverse trends in enrollment at different levels of schooling.

Since the cost per student increases with the level of education (Table 32), it is useful to examine briefly the changes projected over time in the distribution of students at the different school levels (Table 12). By 2025, Canada, France, and the United States will experience a higher enrollment at the preprimary and primary levels, and a decline at the secondary and tertiary levels, compared with 1980. Japan will experience an increase in enrollment at the tertiary level, while at all other educational levels, particularly the preprimary and primary levels, it will register a lower enrollment by 2025, compared with 1980. The decline in the overall enrollment in the United Kingdom between 1980 and 2025 is concentrated at the secondary and tertiary levels, while preprimary enrollment can be expected to be higher at the end of the projection period, compared with 1980. The Federal Republic of Germany, which might have the strongest decline in overall enrollment among the seven major industrial countries, will experience this decline, like the United Kingdom, at the secondary and tertiary levels. How-

Table 12. School Enrollments by Level, as Projected in the Baseline Scenarios, 1980–2025

(Index: 1980 = 100)

Country	1980	2000	2010	2025
Preprimary level				
Canada	100	108	111	113
France	100	108	106	110
Germany, Fed. Rep. of	100	104	85	82
Italy	100	100	88	88
Japan	100	79	85	79
United Kingdom	100	109	103	106
United States	100	107	109	112
Primary level				
Canada	100	110	106	110
France	100	102	97	102
Germany, Fed. Rep. of	100	101	80	76
Italy	100	85	82	76
Japan	100	76	86	79
United Kingdom	100	93	89	90
United States	100	107	102	109
Secondary level				
Canada	100	94	92	94
France	100	100	98	98
Germany, Fed. Rep. of	100	63	64	51
Italy	100	73	83	72
Japan	100	83	92	91
United Kingdom	100	78	82	79
United States	100	100	95	100
Tertiary level				
Canada	100	82	87	83
France	100	82	100	111
Germany, Fed. Rep. of	100	61	70	57
Italy	100	85	85	83
Japan	100	103	90	103
United Kingdom	100	80	86	83
United States	100	85	91	89

Source: Fund staff estimates.

Table 13. Demographic Effect on Education Expenditure, 1980–2025[1]

(Index: 1980 = 100)

Country	1980	2000	2010	2025
		Baseline scenarios		
Canada	100	96	96	97
France	100	98	99	102
Germany, Fed. Rep. of	100	76	72	62
Italy	100	81	83	76
Japan	100	81	88	86
United Kingdom	100	97	89	88
United States	100	95	95	98
		"Greater aging" scenarios		
Canada	100	95	91	85
France	100	95	93	91
Germany, Fed. Rep. of	100	71	63	50
Italy	100	78	74	64
Japan	100	80	81	68
United Kingdom	100	86	83	76
United States	100	90	83	74

Source: Fund staff estimates.
[1] In absolute terms.

ever, in the Federal Republic of Germany, enrollment at these levels will be half the size, compared with 1980, while in the United Kingdom enrollment at these levels will be only 20 percent lower.

In the "greater aging" scenario, the downward trend in enrollment is accentuated relative to the baseline scenario. In the Federal Republic of Germany, school enrollment by 2025 is projected at less than half its 1980 level, while in Italy, Japan, and the United Kingdom, a 30 percent decline in enrollments can be envisioned.

Table 13 illustrates how the development of overall enrollment and the changes in the distribution across educational levels will influence absolute expenditure on education, assuming that costs per student by educational level and educational participation rates remain at their 1980 level. Structural changes in enrollment in France show no impact on overall expenditure. In contrast, in Canada and the United States expenditure on education is projected to be somewhat lower by 2025, compared with 1980, because of lower enrollment at the tertiary level, notwithstanding unchanged overall enrollments. In the Federal Republic of Germany, absolute expenditure will fall more than the overall enrollment level, because enrollment at the secondary and tertiary levels will be markedly lower by 2025 than in 1980. In other countries, the structural changes are not projected to have a significant impact on the level of overall absolute expenditure.

These demographic trends may be expressed in terms of their impact on the ratio of education expenditure to GDP, given assumptions on the likely growth in real educational costs per student over time. With the exception of Japan, it is assumed that the teacher-pupil ratio is held constant at the 1980 level. In Japan, this assumption is made only for the preprimary and tertiary levels of education; at the primary and secondary levels, government policy seeks an increase in the teacher-pupil ratio through the year 1991, such that the ratio of expenditure on primary and secondary education to GDP is assumed constant through that year. Thereafter, the teacher-pupil ratio is assumed to remain constant.

It is also assumed that the cost per student (i.e., salaries, equipment, and supplies) grows at the same rate as productivity in the economy. This last assumption is based on the high labor intensity of the education production function and the limited opportunity for capital-labor substitution. It also reflects the assumption that relative wage rates between teachers and other professions in the economy are unchanged.

No differential is assumed between the growth in cost per student and productivity, as all countries, except the United States, suffer from an excess supply of professionally trained teachers. Thus, in the foreseeable future, it does not appear necessary to offer special incentives to attract secondary school graduates to this field.

By assuming constant teacher-pupil ratios, these projections also effectively assume that a decline in enrollment relative to the size of the labor force is reflected immediately in a reduction of expenditure. However, such an assumption reflects neither the high fixed costs present in the education sector nor the institutional restrictions limiting the ability to lay off teachers. Thus, while these calculations may overstate the potential savings over the next 10–15 years, they might capture the correct trend in the long run or represent the maximum savings that can be achieved over time.

The results suggest that the decline in the expenditure ratio will not be as dramatic as the demographic trends might suggest (Chart 13 and Table 14). In fact, the prospective changes in the expenditure ratios are more similar across countries than are the trends in enrollments because of offsetting trends in the size of the labor force in the different countries. Countries such as France and the United States, which according to the baseline demographic scenario will have the same overall school enrollment by 2025 as in 1980, show a reduction in the ratio of education expenditure to GDP because of an increasing active labor force. In contrast, the Federal Republic of Germany shows a 20 percent savings, although the overall enrollment is projected to be 35 percent lower, because the labor force will drop in size over time. However, despite the decline in enrollment in most countries, savings in terms of GDP turn out to be at best 1 percentage point. In the "greater aging" demographic scenario, because of even lower enrollment levels, savings can be expected in the range of 1.0–1.5 percentage points of GDP.

Policy Issues

The seven major industrial countries do not share the same problems in the field of education, as they are affected differently by demographic developments. Since Canada and France will not face dramatic changes in enrollment in the near future, demographics and education are not a political issue. In Japan, issues of the character and quality of education appear to be far more important in terms of the political agenda. Major changes in the curriculum and examination system are the subject of considerable public discus-

Chart 13. Government Education Expenditure as a Percentage of GDP, 1980–2025

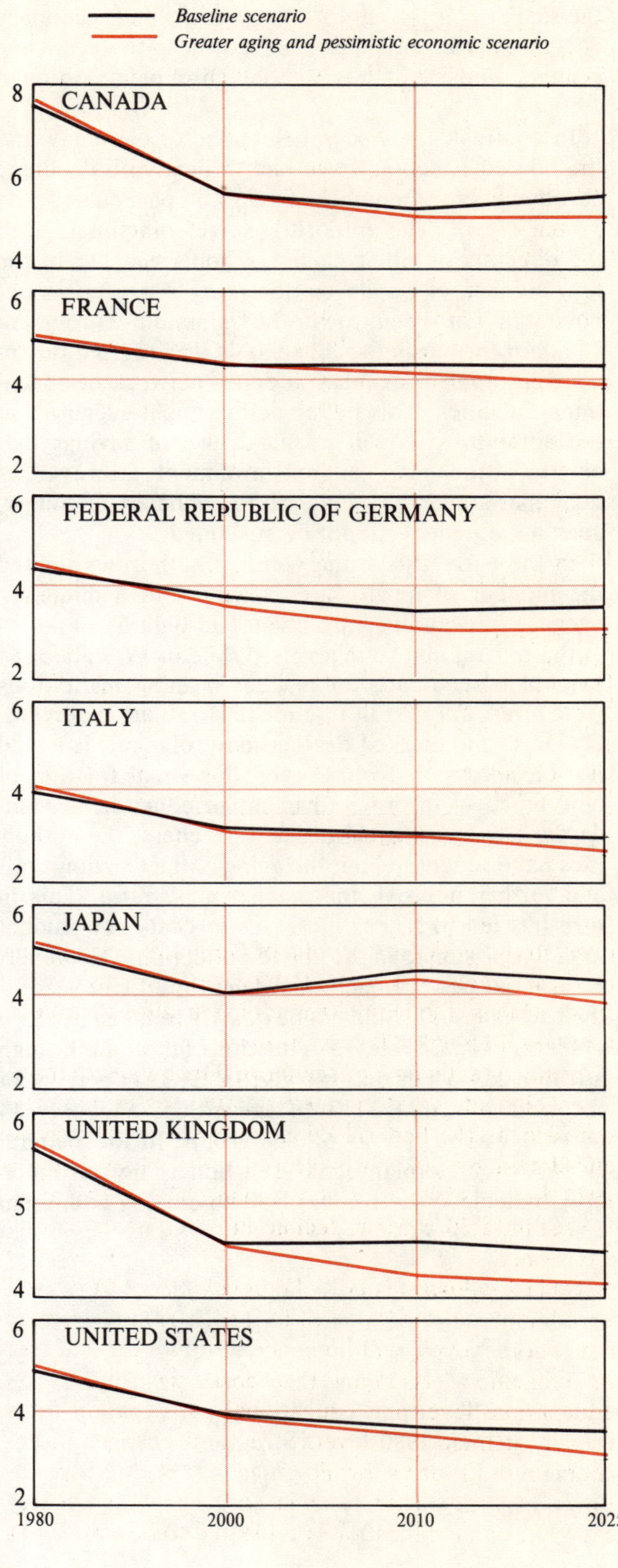

sion. Moreover, Japan has adopted a medium-term policy of raising the teacher-student ratio by about 10 percent for elementary and secondary schools over the 1980–92 period. This underlies the assumption that the share of output allocated to primary and secondary education will remain unchanged, despite decreasing primary and secondary school enrollments through 1991.

In contrast, the Federal Republic of Germany and the United Kingdom have had to deal with declining enrollments for a number of years, in particular at the primary level. The authorities have sometimes faced the dilemma of either closing schools because of the low number of pupils or accepting rising costs per pupil. In both countries, the minimum enrollment standard for closing small schools was revised downward in order to maintain a dense network of educational facilities. This policy action might suggest that the authorities would not make use of savings that emerge at times of declining enrollment. However, as demonstrated in the Federal Republic of Germany, such an argument cannot be sustained.

In the early 1980s, the German authorities limited the number of newly hired teachers to a minimum because of declining enrollment and tight fiscal policy at the federal and state levels. While in 1979 about 84 percent of graduates of teacher training institutions were hired, in 1983 this fraction fell to about 25 percent. Owing to the marked decline in enrollment, it would not be necessary to hire even this small fraction of new teachers in order to maintain educational standards. However, by hiring new teachers, the authorities have sought to limit the aging of the teaching staff and further improve the teacher-pupil ratio. This in turn has led to higher increases in costs per student than was assumed in the above projections. However, even if no new teachers had been hired, the size of the teaching staff could not be quickly reduced because of lifetime tenure rules. A reduction of the staff through attrition can occur only slowly. In 1983, 44 percent of the staff was in the 30–40 age group, and only 14 percent was in the 50–65 age group. In the Federal Republic of Germany, the question is not so much how to achieve savings but how to employ additional staff without exceeding budgetary limits—a seemingly impossible goal as the status quo of salaries and benefits of the existing staff is considered inviolable.

In Italy, the adjustment problem is more difficult because of the strong unionization of teachers. Owing to pressure from labor unions, all auxiliary teachers were made regular staff with lifetime tenure some years ago. Furthermore, teachers receive indexation adjustments to their salaries twice a year. This means that, contrary to the assumptions made for Italy, cost increases are likely to exceed productivity growth and inflation.

In the United States, the problems are of a different kind. In the 1970s, initial declines in enrollment were not matched by a reduction in the number of teachers employed. This did not occur until the late 1970s, and was also accompanied by an erosion of remuneration. In 1982, the annual supply of newly qualified teachers fell by half relative to 1970. If students continue to choose careers in other fields because of perceived better salaries and working conditions, a shortage of new teachers is expected to emerge by the end of the 1980s, when the decline in enrollment will bottom out. This shortage might lead to a marked upgrading of teacher remuneration that will increase costs in the education sector above the assumed levels.

Apart from the individual problems that the countries face, some common challenges are likely to emerge. For example, it has often been argued that the real cost of stagnant or declining enrollment is a reduction in the number of new faculty hirings. Since in some countries (e.g., the United States), new faculty at the tertiary level of education are responsible for much research, this could have some effect on the rate of technological progress. Another such challenge might be an increase in the demand for adult education, which might absorb some of the projected savings in education expenditure. These examples show that the assumptions made in the projections may turn out to be optimistic regarding the savings that can emerge in the education sector because of future demographic developments. If there are savings, they are likely to be small and will compensate only to a limited extent for rising costs in other social expenditure categories.

VII Unemployment Compensation, Family Benefits, and Other Social Programs: Projections and Policy Issues

Unemployment Compensation

Although the level of unemployment is clearly a major determinant of expenditure on unemployment compensation programs, the correspondence is less than perfect. Thus, while the level of unemployment in the seven major industrial countries was about 7 million in 1960, almost 13 million in 1975, 15 million in 1980, and peaked at 23 million in 1983, real expenditure has evolved rather differently (Table 1). Between 1960 and 1975 real expenditure grew nearly three times as fast as the level of unemployment, while program coverage was expanded and average real benefits increased. In contrast, between 1975 and 1981 real expenditure was outpaced by the growth of the level of unemployment despite increasing average real benefits, because program coverage declined.

The first period, at least up to 1974, was one of genuine program expansion, with discretionary improvement in coverage and benefit levels. Unemployment was fairly stable. But in 1975, in the aftermath of the first oil shock, unemployment rose dramatically, moderated slightly by 1979, and then rose again after the second oil shock. To understand why the marked increase in unemployment between 1975 and 1981 had a more limited impact on expenditure, it is necessary to describe the structure of unemployment compensation programs.

Basically, unemployment compensation programs are designed to help those with a previous record of employment who are expected to return to work within a relatively short time after becoming unemployed. Thus, the programs pay earnings-related benefits for a limited period of time.[64] The payment period is usually a year or less, although in France and the Federal Republic of Germany it is longer for older workers. In some countries (e.g., Canada and the Federal Republic of Germany), the eligibility period varies with the length of previous employment. After eligibility for unemployment benefits runs out, only welfare benefits are available to the unemployed.

It has been noted that between 1975 and 1981 the increase in the level of unemployment was accompanied by an increase in average real benefits. In contrast to the previous period, this reflected not so much discretionary increases in benefit levels—indeed, concern about the supply-side impact of these programs actually led to discretionary reductions in benefit levels in some countries—but the successively higher levels of earnings on which benefits were based as unemployment began to affect individuals in increasingly better paid jobs.

The fall in coverage that accompanied increasing unemployment in part reflects a tightening of eligibility criteria, but this was relatively minor. It is principally a reflection of a change in the composition of the unemployed, with those less likely to be covered by unemployment compensation forming an increasingly large share of the total. Youth unemployment and long-term unemployment are now of significant magnitude. The young usually have no previous employment record that would establish a claim to unemployment compensation; the long-term unemployed will normally have exhausted any claim they previously held. Married women also represent a disproportionate number of the unemployed; they are not adequately covered by unemployment compensation because of their often incomplete employment records.[65]

Even with some knowledge of the likely evolution of the level of unemployment, because of the complex way in which the level of unemployment, coverage, and benefit levels interact, speculation about the future development of expenditure on unemployment compensation is particularly hazardous. When account is

[64] The only country not providing earnings-related benefits is the United Kingdom, although it did so between 1974 and 1981. These benefits were discontinued in 1982.

[65] Roberti (1984) provides a detailed discussion of the underlying changes in expenditure on unemployment compensation programs in the seven major industrial countries.

taken of the enormous difficulty in forming any reasonable view of trends in unemployment over the next ten years, let alone over the next 40, an attempt to project long-term expenditure on unemployment compensation programs looks like an exercise in futility—but this does not make it any less necessary. In order to build a complete picture of the future development of social expenditure, some illustrative numbers are necessary. Because unemployment compensation is a small program in expenditure terms, projected trends in overall social expenditure are not sensitive to what it is reasonable to assume about expenditure on unemployment compensation. Thus, the approach taken here is relatively mechanical and simple.

It will be recalled that the economic scenarios described in Chapter II embody assumptions about future unemployment rates. These tend to be ad hoc assumptions, reflecting in the baseline scenario some retreat from the peak unemployment rates of 1983 to long-term rates close to those experienced immediately prior to the second oil shock, and reflecting in the pessimistic economic scenario not the peak 1983 rates but those experienced at the beginning of the recession.[66] These unemployment rates form the basis of the expenditure projections described below. As regards coverage, it is assumed that this is held at its 1980 level, while benefits increase with average productivity (or GDP per capita in the case of the United Kingdom).

Chart 14 and Table 14 trace the development of the ratio of expenditure on unemployment compensation to GDP over the projection period, highlighting the effect of the range of assumptions about future unemployment, with, in the baseline scenario, France at the optimistic end of the range and Italy at the pessimistic end. In the Federal Republic of Germany, the results may also appear to be at the optimistic end, until account is taken of the marked fall in the size of the labor force. As the pessimistic economic scenario is characterized by higher unemployment rates than the baseline scenario, it thus shows higher expenditure ratios.

Although unemployment compensation programs are small and will probably remain so in expenditure terms, the policy issues with which they are associated are equally as important as those associated with the much larger programs in pensions, medical care, and education. Furthermore, they are of more immediate importance. It has been widely argued that supply-side rigidities, particularly in the labor market, have been holding back growth, especially in Europe. A range of such rigidities has been identified, including

[66] See Chapter II for details of the assumptions made for each country.

Chart 14. Government Expenditure on Unemployment Compensation as a Percentage of GDP, 1980–2025

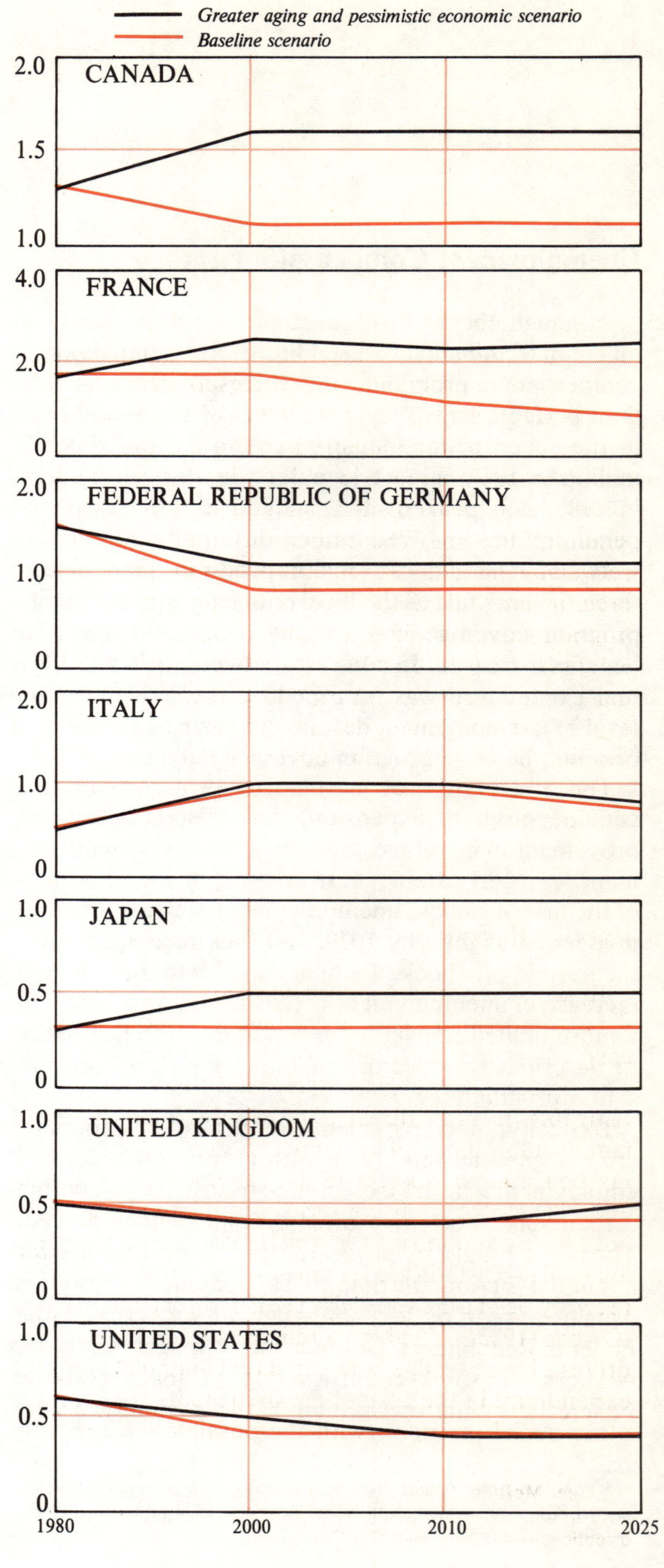

wage-fixing mechanisms, legislation governing the hiring and firing of labor, and unemployment compensation provisions.

As regards the last, the view has been formed that unemployment compensation programs designed to deal with the frictional and cyclical unemployment of the 1950s, 1960s, and early 1970s have proven inadequate under modern labor market conditions characterized by high levels of structural unemployment. These programs therefore need redesigning, with the emphasis being taken away from compensation of the short-term unemployed. Instead, these individuals might be integrated into a wider program of retraining and relocation better suited to their needs as well as those of the wider labor market.[67]

As pointed out, this ongoing debate may be of critical short-term importance, but it also has long-term significance. Anticipated demographic developments are going to affect the size and the sex and age composition of the work force. They will also affect the demand side, changing patterns of demand for goods and services that will feed through to the derived demand for labor. The outcome could be major labor market mismatches, resolvable only if the labor market is sufficiently flexible, thus requiring greater substitutability among different demographic groups. For example, women may have to move into traditionally male-dominated occupations; older workers may have to fill jobs that have previously been the preserve of the young. Unemployment compensation could be an integral part of a labor market adjustment mechanism that can help overcome the problems created by supply and demand mismatches.

Family Benefits

In the seven major industrial countries, both direct expenditures and tax concessions are used to provide cash assistance to families with dependent children. The Federal Republic of Germany and the United Kingdom rely on direct expenditure in the form of family allowances. The United States provides only tax concessions (except in the case of welfare recipients). The other four countries offer a combination of both. In two countries for which information is readily available—Canada and France—tax expenditure has recently been a little less than half of direct expenditure (Owens (1983)). The heavy reliance on tax expenditure drives a larger wedge between direct and total effective expenditure in the case of family benefits than for any other social program (with the possible exception of

[67] See McBain (1984) and Reyher and Spitznagel (1984) for descriptions of some actual and potential developments in this direction.

Chart 15. Family Benefits as a Percentage of GDP, 1980–2025

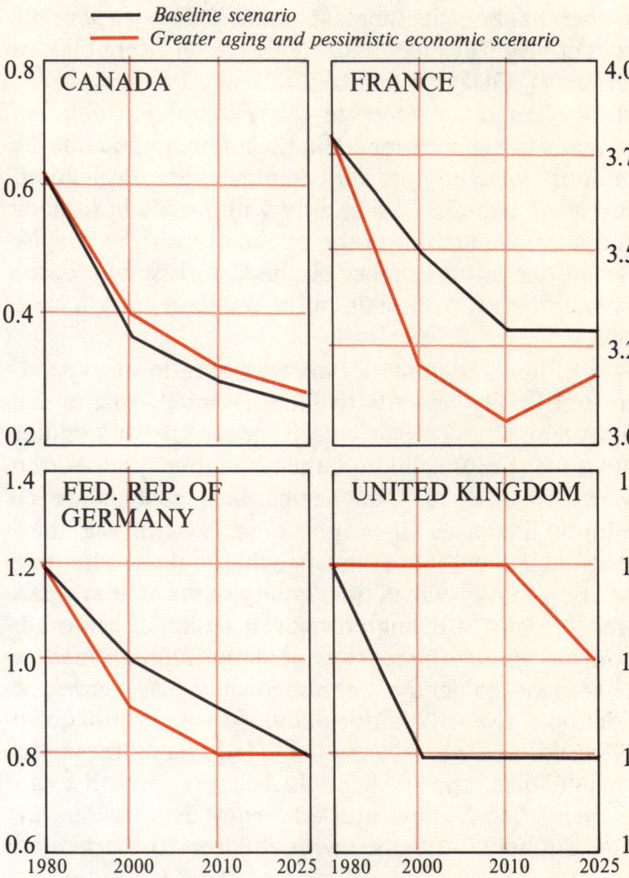

housing). This being so, projections of social expenditure on family benefits are probably a poor guide to the total expenditure on cash assistance to families with dependent children.[68]

The projections presented in Chart 15 and Table 14 refer to direct social expenditure on family benefits alone. Thus, there are no figures for the United States, since there is no such expenditure item. In addition, this category of expenditure has not been separately identified in Italy and Japan, although it is incorporated

[68] However, as discussed in Chapter II, there is an issue as to whether tax expenditures can be equated with direct expenditures, since the objectives of the two types of expenditure might be quite different. As Owens (1983, p. 176) points out, it has to be decided "whether a particular tax provision is a tax expenditure, and therefore a substitute for an expenditure provision, or an integral part of the income tax system designed to measure taxable capacity." It is probably fair to say that child tax allowances were originally put in place to fulfill fiscal objectives, but as the coverage of the income tax has extended further down the income scale, they have been increasingly important as instruments of social policy. Detailed descriptions of the total cash assistance to families with dependent children in a number of countries, including most of the seven major industrial countries, can be found in Kahn and Kamerman (1983).

in the projections in a residual expenditure category ("other social expenditure"). In the remaining four countries, the projections reflect anticipated trends in the number of qualifying children. The projections assume that benefits increase in line only with average productivity (France and the Federal Republic of Germany), GDP per capita (the United Kingdom), or prices (Canada).[69] Only in the Federal Republic of Germany is a significant fall in the number of qualifying children expected, and this dominates the projection. Increasing benefits in line only with prices in Canada produces a reduction in the expenditure ratio despite a slight rise in the number of children. Elsewhere, the expenditure ratios remain fairly stable under all scenarios.

With the exception of France, the ratio of expenditure on family benefits to GDP is small. In France, family benefits are particularly generous for families with three or more children, the belief (partly supported by evidence) being that the marginal cost of raising children increases disproportionately with the third child and that without assistance this could be a limiting factor on family size. Thus, family benefits are in part a reflection of a strong pronatalist tendency. In other countries, family benefits principally fulfill an income maintenance objective, although they also serve the wider objectives of family policy. However, pronatalist objectives are typically not included among these. As a result, discussions of family benefits tend to focus on their effectiveness and efficiency in providing income support to families with children. In particular, the nature and extent of support provided to single-parent families has been a growing concern as the numbers of such families have recently been increasing faster than ever before.

Other Social Expenditure

Chart 16 illustrates projected developments in expenditure on a composite group of smaller social programs (see also Table 14).[70] It is assumed that

Chart 16. Other Government Social Expenditure as a Percentage of GDP, 1980–2025

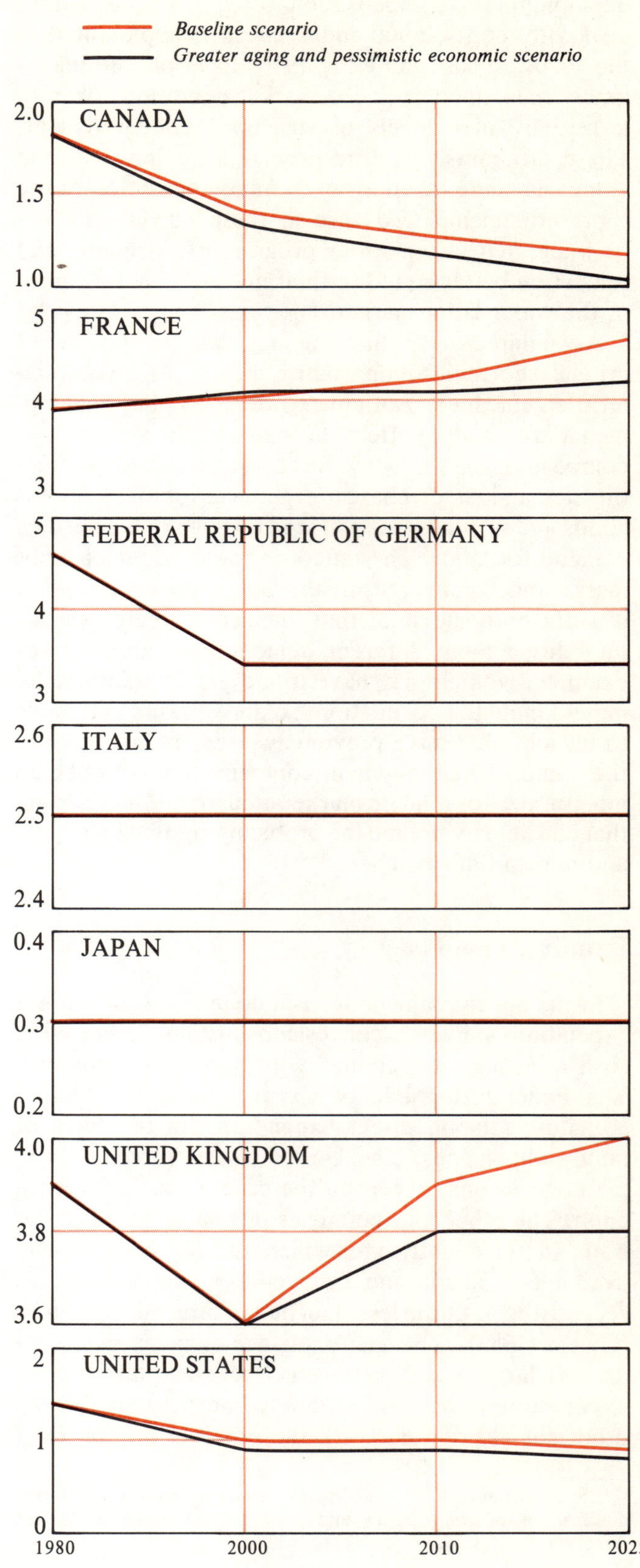

[69] The "prices" assumption in Canada reflects existing policy. This policy exists also in the United Kingdom, although a more generous provision is built into the projections.

[70] The programs included are indicated as follows:

(1) *Canada:* expenditure on the Canada Assistance Plan, sickness, maternity, veterans' affairs, and Indian affairs.

(2) *France:* maternity, training, and work-related accident benefits, and administrative costs. In the baseline case the projections are to 2020 only.

(3) *Germany, Federal Republic of:* welfare and social services, special compensations (including veterans' payments, land-loss compensation, and political compensation), and workmen's compensation benefits.

(4) *Italy:* family and workmen's compensation benefits.

(5) *Japan:* disability and welfare benefits.

benefits increase either with average productivity (France and the Federal Republic of Germany), GDP per capita (Italy, Japan, and the United Kingdom), prices (Canada), or prices plus 1 percent (United States).

It is difficult to discuss expenditure growth, its causes, and the associated policy issues for a composite of a disparate group of benefits like those included in the "other social expenditure" category. However, it should be noted that in no country is the ratio of expenditure to GDP devoted to these benefits, taken together, lower than the ratio of expenditure on unemployment compensation; and in Canada, the Federal Republic of Germany, and the United Kingdom, it is larger than the sum of the unemployment compensation and family benefit ratios. In the Federal Republic of Germany, it actually exceeds the education ratio. Thus, in expenditure terms, this group of benefits is far from trivial, although no individual program included in the group is likely to be of any significant size.

(6) *United Kingdom:* disability, sickness, widows' and supplementary benefits, and administrative costs.

(7) *United States:* expenditure on food and nutrition programs and low-income programs (e.g., aid to families with dependent children) administered by the Department of Health and Human Services.

Appendix I

Statistical Tables

Table 14. Social Expenditure Under Alternative Economic and Demographic Scenarios, 1980–2025

(As a percentage of GDP)

		Baseline Economic and Demographic Scenario			Baseline Economic and "Greater Aging" Scenario			Pessimistic Economic and "Greater Aging" Scenario		
	1980	2000	2010	2025	2000	2010	2025	2000	2010	2025
Canada										
Medical care[1]	5.55	5.93	6.45	8.44	5.84	6.33	8.39	5.99	6.50	8.63
Pensions	3.50	3.10	3.10	4.30	3.10	3.20	4.50	3.40	3.60	5.30
Education	7.47	5.56	5.32	5.60	5.30	4.84	4.84	5.48	5.00	5.00
Subtotal	*16.52*	*14.59*	*14.87*	*18.34*	*14.24*	*14.37*	*17.73*	*14.87*	*15.10*	*18.93*
Unemployment	1.33	1.06	1.06	1.06	1.06	1.06	1.06	1.64	1.64	1.64
Family benefits	0.62	0.37	0.30	0.26	0.38	0.30	0.26	0.39	0.31	0.27
Other	1.82	1.33	1.17	1.03	1.36	1.22	1.12	1.40	1.26	1.16
Total	**20.29**	**17.35**	**17.40**	**20.69**	**17.03**	**16.95**	**20.18**	**18.30**	**18.31**	**22.00**
France										
Medical care[1]	6.70	7.70	8.25	9.38	7.44	8.10	10.21	7.60	8.40	10.70
Pensions	10.00	11.00	11.50	13.00	10.80	12.20	15.60	11.00	12.60	16.30
Education	4.90	4.44	4.36	4.39	4.21	3.95	3.76	4.30	4.10	3.94
Subtotal	*21.60*	*23.14*	*24.11*	*26.77*	*22.45*	*24.25*	*29.56*	*22.90*	*25.10*	*30.94*
Unemployment	1.70	1.70	1.10	0.80	1.65	1.10	0.80	2.48	2.28	2.35
Family benefits	3.80	3.50	3.30	3.30	3.10	2.90	3.00	3.20	3.06	3.18
Other	3.90	4.10	4.10	4.20	3.90	4.00	4.40	4.03	4.22	4.66
Total	**31.00**	**32.44**	**32.61**	**35.07**	**31.10**	**32.25**	**37.76**	**32.61**	**34.66**	**41.13**
Germany, Fed. Rep. of										
Medical care[1]	6.10	7.10	8.10	9.70	7.03	8.02	9.90	7.10	8.10	10.00
Pensions	13.30	17.10	18.60	20.50	17.10	18.80	21.20	17.10	18.80	21.10
Education	4.38	3.75	3.50	3.57	3.44	3.00	2.98	3.47	3.03	3.01
Subtotal	*23.78*	*27.95*	*30.20*	*33.77*	*27.57*	*29.82*	*34.08*	*27.67*	*29.93*	*34.11*
Unemployment	1.50	0.80	0.80	0.80	0.80	0.80	0.80	1.10	1.10	1.10
Family benefits	1.20	1.00	0.90	0.80	0.90	0.80	0.70	0.90	0.80	0.80
Other	4.60	3.40	3.40	3.40	3.40	3.40	3.40	3.40	3.40	3.40
Total	**31.08**	**33.15**	**35.30**	**38.77**	**32.67**	**34.82**	**38.98**	**33.07**	**35.23**	**39.41**
Italy										
Medical care[1]	5.96	6.47	7.01	7.76	6.48	7.09	8.14	6.54	7.13	8.16
Pensions	12.10	14.60	16.70	20.70	14.90	17.60	23.00	15.10	17.70	23.10
Education	4.00	3.20	3.10	3.00	2.97	2.88	2.59	3.00	2.90	2.60
Subtotal	*22.06*	*24.27*	*26.81*	*31.46*	*24.35*	*27.57*	*33.73*	*24.64*	*27.73*	*33.86*
Unemployment	0.50	0.90	0.90	0.70	0.90	0.90	0.80	1.00	0.97	0.83
Family benefits	—	—	—	—	—	—	—	—	—	—
Other	2.50	2.50	2.50	2.50	2.50	2.50	2.50	2.50	2.50	2.50
Total	**25.06**	**27.67**	**30.21**	**34.66**	**27.75**	**30.97**	**37.03**	**28.14**	**31.20**	**37.19**

Table 14 (*concluded*). Social Expenditure Under Alternative Economic and Demographic Scenarios, 1980–2025

(As a percentage of GDP)

		Baseline Economic and Demographic Scenario			Baseline Economic and "Greater Aging" Scenario			Pessimistic Economic and "Greater Aging" Scenario		
	1980	2000	2010	2025	2000	2010	2025	2000	2010	2025
Japan										
Medical care[1]	4.80	6.05	7.08	8.06	6.21	7.24	8.35	6.27	7.31	8.43
Pensions	4.20	9.61	12.89	13.40	10.38	14.28	15.30	10.49	14.40	15.50
Education	5.10	4.10	4.60	4.40	3.97	4.26	3.77	4.00	4.30	3.80
Subtotal	*14.10*	*19.76*	*24.56*	*25.86*	*20.56*	*25.78*	*27.42*	*20.76*	*26.00*	*27.73*
Unemployment	0.30	0.30	0.30	0.30	0.30	0.30	0.30	0.45	0.45	0.45
Family benefits	—	—	—	—	—	—	—	—	—	—
Other	1.00	1.00	1.00	1.00	1.00	1.00	1.00	1.00	1.00	1.00
Total	**15.40**	**21.06**	**25.86**	**27.16**	**21.86**	**27.08**	**28.72**	**22.21**	**27.45**	**29.18**
United Kingdom										
Medical care[1]	5.80	6.59	6.84	8.35	6.59	7.04	8.85	6.59	7.04	8.85
Pensions	5.80	6.65	7.22	8.36	6.85	7.66	9.34	6.85	7.66	9.34
Education	5.60	4.60	4.60	4.50	4.50	4.20	4.10	4.50	4.20	4.10
Subtotal	*17.20*	*17.84*	*18.66*	*21.22*	*17.93*	*18.90*	*22.29*	*17.93*	*18.90*	*22.29*
Unemployment	0.50	0.40	0.40	0.40	0.40	0.40	0.50	0.40	0.40	0.50
Family benefits	1.30	1.10	1.10	1.10	1.30	1.30	1.20	1.30	1.30	1.20
Other	3.90	3.60	3.80	3.80	3.60	3.90	4.00	3.60	3.90	4.00
Total	**22.90**	**22.94**	**23.96**	**26.52**	**23.23**	**24.50**	**27.99**	**23.23**	**24.50**	**27.99**
United States										
Medical care[1]	4.50	5.39	5.84	7.76	5.54	6.24	8.75	5.57	6.27	8.80
Pensions	6.30	5.80	5.70	6.90	6.00	6.10	7.90	6.40	6.60	8.50
Education	4.87	3.95	3.73	3.58	3.77	3.36	2.95	3.80	3.38	2.97
Subtotal	*15.67*	*15.14*	*15.27*	*18.24*	*15.31*	*15.70*	*19.60*	*15.77*	*16.25*	*20.27*
Unemployment	0.60	0.40	0.40	0.40	0.40	0.40	0.40	0.50	0.40	0.40
Family benefits	—	—	—	—	—	—	—	—	—	—
Other	1.40	0.90	0.90	0.80	0.90	0.80	0.70	1.00	1.00	0.90
Total	**17.67**	**16.44**	**16.57**	**19.44**	**16.61**	**16.90**	**20.70**	**17.27**	**17.65**	**21.57**

Sources: For 1980, see references to Table 15. Projections are based on Fund staff estimates.

[1] Includes expenditure on medical administration, medical research and education, and capital expenditure.

Table 15. Government Social Expenditure Ratios by Sector, 1980

(As a percentage of GDP)

Country	Education	Total Medical Expenditure	Of Which: Personal medical expenditure	Pensions[1]	Unemployment Insurance	Other Social Expenditure	Total
Canada[2]	7.5	5.6	(4.4)	3.5	1.5	2.2	20.3
France[3]	4.9	6.7	(...)	10.0	1.7	7.7	31.0
Germany, Fed. Rep. of[4]	4.4	6.1	(6.1)	13.3	1.5	5.8	31.1
Italy[5]	4.0	5.9	(4.9)	12.1	0.5	2.5	25.0
Japan[6]	5.1	4.8	(...)	4.2	0.3	1.0	15.4
United Kingdom[7]	5.6	5.8	(5.5)	5.8	0.5	5.2	22.9
United States[8]	4.9	4.5	(3.3)	6.3	0.6	1.4	17.7

Sources:

Canada: Canadian Tax Foundation (1982); and Katz (1985).

France: IRES (1983); Ministère de l'Economie, des Finances et du Budget (1984); and Nivollet (1985).

Germany (Federal Republic): Bundesminister für Arbeit und Sozialordnung (1983, 1984a, 1984b); and Kohnert (1985).

Italy: ISTAT (1983); and Ruggiero (1985).

Japan: Prime Minister's Office, Bureau of Statistics (1983); Kenko Hoken Kumiai Rengookai (1984); and Feldman (1985).

United Kingdom: H.M. Treasury (1984); and Mansur (1985).

United States: Gibson and others (1984); U.S. Department of Education, National Center for Education Statistics (1984); Council of Economic Advisers (1985); and McDonald (1985).

[1] In France, Italy, and the United States, includes disability and survivors' benefits.

[2] "Other Social Expenditure" includes family allowances, the Canada Assistance Plan, Veterans' Benefits, and Indian Affairs; pensions include the Old Age Security program and pensions under the Canada Pension Plan and the Quebec Pension Plan.

[3] "Other Social Expenditure" includes disability and death benefits, family benefits, training activities, work-related accident benefits, and administration. Social expenditures include, in addition to social benefits to resident households, benefits to nonresidents, nonindividualized social services, management expenses, tax benefits, and nonclassified expenditure. The other categories of benefits other than social benefits to resident households are approximately 13 percent of the total.

[4] "Other Social Expenditure" includes workmen's compensation, children's allowances, welfare benefits, special compensations (veterans' payments, land loss compensation, political compensation, etc.). Pensions include pensions under the general social security system, pensions under the special social security system, civil service benefits, and supplementary pensions for public employees. Medical expenditure excludes budgetary expenditure on capital expenditure in health, medical education, and medical research, for lack of available data.

[5] "Other Social Expenditure" includes welfare benefits, other social security benefits (including sickness and temporary disability benefits), maternity benefits, salary compensation, family allowances, retirement lump-sum benefits). Medical expenditure is inclusive of administrative costs and capital expenditure. Total expenditure is inclusive of administrative costs and capital expenditure in the various sectors.

[6] "Other Social Expenditure" includes miscellaneous central and local government expenditure on social-welfare-related programs (such as child care, disability, livelihood protection, outlays on the indigent, etc.). Educational expenditure includes assumed government subsidy rate of 25 percent for private educational expenditure per student (see Japan, Bureau of Statistics (1985), p. 580).

[7] "Other Social Expenditure" includes sickness benefits, invalid benefits, industrial injuries benefits, maternity benefits, widows' benefits, and various noncontributory benefits (such as a supplementary allowance, war pensions, and administrative costs).

[8] Pensions include survivors' and disability pensions and some welfare components. They exclude pension disbursements to retired state and local government employees. "Other Social Expenditure" includes the food and nutrition programs of the Department of Agriculture and various programs administered by the Department of Health and Human Services (including aid to families with dependent children, social services block grants, low-income energy assistance, earned income tax credit, and refugee assistance). Medical expenditure includes other expenditures on health (including administration, public health activities, research, and construction).

Table 16. Overall Social Expenditure Ratios by Sector, 1980[1]

(As a percentage of GDP)

Country	Education	Medical Care	Pensions	Unemployment Insurance	Other	Subtotal	Tax Expenditure[2]	Total
Canada[3]	8.1	7.5	4.8	1.5	2.2	24.2	0.3	24.4
France	4.9	8.0	10.0	1.7	7.7	32.3	1.6	33.9
Germany, Fed. Rep. of[4]	4.4	8.7	13.3	1.5	5.8	33.7	0.2	33.9
Italy[5]	4.0	6.8	12.1	0.5	2.5	25.9	. . .	25.9[6]
Japan	6.3	5.0	4.2	0.3	1.0	16.8	. . .	16.8[6]
United Kingdom	5.6	5.8	9.0	0.5	5.2	26.1	1.0	27.1
United States[7]	6.6	9.5	8.1	0.6	1.4	26.2	2.0	28.2

Sources: Table 15 and specific country sources mentioned in the footnotes.

[1] See footnotes in Table 15. Overall social expenditure in this table includes tax expenditures for social programs, private sector expenditures on education and medical care, and private pension plan disbursements.

[2] In the United Kingdom, tax expenditure relates to the tax relief for pension schemes and self-employed retirement annuity payments, unemployment and sickness benefits, invalid benefits, and statutory redundancy benefits. In France, diverse tax relief is provided in the form of aid to the aged, the "défavorisés," and the family. These are listed and, where possible, quantified in France, Ministry of Finance (1985). In the Federal Republic of Germany, there are only limited tax expenditures. In Canada, statistics on tax expenditure are provided by the authorities and included in *Government of Canada Tax Expenditure Accounts* (1980). In the United States, tax expenditure includes the exclusion of employer contributions for medical insurance premiums and health care and deductibility of medical expenses, exemptions for social security, workmen's compensation and unemployment benefits, exclusion of other employee benefits, the additional exemption for the elderly, exclusion of veterans' disability compensation, and various exemptions related to education (see United States, Executive Office of the President, Office of Management and Budget, *Special Analyses* (1985)). Not included as tax expenditures are personal exemptions and standard deductions, which serve as much to increase the degree of progressivity associated with an income tax as to give a benefit to families. For additional information on tax expenditures, see McDaniel and Surrey (1985).

[3] Includes $3.9 billion in private pension expenditure to pension recipients in 1980; does not include $0.4 billion in annuity incomes from Canadian equivalent of Individual Retirement Accounts (IRAs). Source: Canada, Department of Finance (1980).

[4] Based on a 1975 estimate that government expenditure on medical care (as in Table 15) excluded expenditure by private households for nonprescription drugs, government expenditure for capital investments in hospitals, medical schools, and medical research, as well as expenditures made by private insurance funds. These other categories of medical expenditure represented 30 percent of the total medical care bill (U.S. concept). Tax expenditures are based on a generous interpretation that tax expenditures on "other" fall within the category of social expenditure.

[5] Based on a Fund staff estimate that 86.5 percent of national health and medical expenditure is covered by government expenditure (Ruggiero (1985)).

[6] Excluding tax expenditure.

[7] Private pension statistics derived from Munnell (1982, p. 11). These statistics also include pensions of state and local government employees.

Table 17. Government Social Expenditure: Comparison of OECD and IMF Estimates, 1980

(Expenditure as a percentage of GDP)

Country	Social Expenditure		Health		Education		Pensions	
	OECD	IMF	OECD	IMF	OECD	IMF	OECD	IMF
Canada	21.0	20.3	5.4	5.6	6.0	7.5	4.4	3.5
France	28.3	31.0	6.1	6.7	5.7	4.9	11.5	10.0
Germany, Fed. Rep. of	30.8	31.9	6.5	6.1	5.1	5.2	12.4	13.3
Italy	26.8	25.0	6.0	5.9	5.6	4.0	11.8	12.1
Japan	16.9	15.4	4.6	4.8	5.0	5.1	4.4	4.2
United Kingdom	22.0	22.9	5.2	5.8	5.6	5.6	6.7	5.8
United States	20.7	17.7	4.1	4.5	5.7	4.9	7.2	6.3

Sources: OECD, *Social Expenditure: 1960–1990, Problems of Growth and Control* (1985); and Fund staff estimates.

Table 18. Government Social Expenditure, 1960–81

	Social Expenditure				Expenditure Shares as a Percentage of GDP					
	Expenditure shares as a percentage of GDP		Income elasticity		Health		Education		Pensions	
Country	1960	1981	1960–75	1975–81	1960	1981	1960	1981	1960	1981
Canada	12.1	21.5	1.8	0.9	2.4	5.6	3.0	6.2	2.8	4.6
France	13.4[1]	29.5	1.6	2.2	2.5	6.5	. . .	5.7	5.9	11.9
Germany, Fed. Rep. of	20.5	31.5	1.8	0.8	3.1	6.5	2.4	5.2	9.8	12.5
Italy	16.8	29.1	1.7	1.6	3.2	6.0	3.7	6.4	5.5	13.2
Japan	8.0	17.5	1.6	1.8	1.3	4.7	4.0	5.0	1.4	4.8
United Kingdom	13.9	27.7	2.2	1.8	3.4	5.4	3.7	5.8	4.1	7.4
United States	10.9	20.8	2.4	1.0	1.3	4.2	3.6	5.5	4.2	7.4

Source: OECD, *Social Expenditure: 1960–1990, Problems of Growth and Control* (1985).
[1] Excluding education.

Table 19. Assumed Demographic Parameters, 1980–2025

		Baseline Scenario			"Greater Aging" Scenario		
	1980	2000	2010	2025	2000	2010	2025
Life expectancy at birth: Males				*(In number of years)*			
Canada	71.2	74.1	76.0	78.3	74.1	76.0	78.3
France	71.0	70.0	70.0	70.0	73.2	74.9	77.5
Germany, Fed. Rep. of	69.9	71.3	72.0	73.1	72.7	74.2	76.4
Italy	71.1	72.6	73.2	74.0	74.0	75.5	77.0
Japan	73.6	75.0	75.1	75.1	78.0	78.0	78.0
United Kingdom	71.0	72.6	74.1	76.2	74.0	76.6	79.5
United States	69.9	73.7	74.2	75.0	75.2	76.3	78.0
Average	*71.1*	*72.8*	*73.5*	*74.5*	*74.4*	*75.9*	*77.8*
Life expectancy at birth: Females				*(In number of years)*			
Canada	78.8	79.8	80.5	81.5	79.8	80.5	81.5
France	79.0	78.0	78.0	78.0	79.6	80.2	81.0
Germany, Fed. Rep. of	76.6	78.1	78.9	80.1	79.6	81.3	83.8
Italy	77.8	79.4	80.2	81.0	81.0	81.7	82.5
Japan	79.0	80.4	80.4	80.4	82.3	82.3	82.3
United Kingdom	77.0	78.1	78.8	79.9	79.2	80.8	82.5
United States	77.5	81.1	81.7	82.5	82.7	83.9	85.7
Average	*78.0*	*79.3*	*79.8*	*80.5*	*80.6*	*81.5*	*82.8*
Fertility rates							
Canada	1.81	1.90	2.05	2.05	1.81	1.81	1.81
France	1.87[1]	2.10	2.10	2.10	1.95	1.95	1.95
Germany, Fed. Rep. of	1.42	1.65	1.65	1.65	1.40	1.40	1.40
Italy	1.60	1.90	1.90	1.90	1.65	1.65	1.65
Japan	1.75	1.85	2.00	2.10	1.72	1.72	1.72
United Kingdom	1.78	1.92	2.05	2.08	1.80	1.80	1.80
United States	1.86	1.96	2.00	2.00	1.68	1.60	1.60

Source: Fund staff estimates.
[1] Average 1982–83.

Table 20. Demographic Structure of the Population, 1980–2025
(In percent)

		Baseline Scenario			"Greater Aging" Scenario		
	1980	2000	2010	2025	2000	2010	2025
Share of population aged 65 and over							
Canada	9.5	11.4	12.7	19.3	11.8	13.4	20.8
France	14.0	14.0	13.6	15.8	14.3	14.6	19.3
Germany, Fed. Rep. of	15.5	17.0	20.7	23.6	17.3	21.4	25.4
Italy	13.5	15.7	16.6	19.0	16.2	17.8	21.5
Japan	9.0	14.9	18.2	21.2	17.4	21.4	25.2
United Kingdom	14.8	15.1	15.8	18.5	15.5	16.8	20.8
United States	11.2	13.0	13.8	19.4	13.8	15.4	23.1
Average	*12.5*	*14.4*	*15.9*	*19.5*	*15.2*	*17.3*	*22.3*
Standard deviation	*2.1*	*1.2*	*2.3*	*2.2*	*1.3*	*2.5*	*2.1*
Aged 75 and over							
Canada	3.6	4.5	5.0	7.3	4.8	5.5	8.0
France	5.7	5.7	6.4	5.8	5.8	6.4	8.1
Germany, Fed. Rep. of	6.0	7.0	8.3	10.0	7.0	8.5	11.0
Italy	4.8	6.2	7.1	8.3	6.4	7.7	9.7
Japan	3.1	5.2	7.3	10.5	7.0	9.9	13.7
United Kingdom	5.6	6.7	6.6	7.8	7.0	7.3	9.4
United States	4.5	6.5	6.6	8.4	7.0	7.7	10.6
Average	*4.8*	*6.0*	*6.8*	*8.3*	*6.4*	*7.6*	*10.1*
Standard deviation	*1.0*	*0.8*	*0.9*	*1.5*	*0.8*	*1.3*	*1.8*
Aged 0 to 14							
Canada	23.0	20.6	19.2	18.7	19.9	17.6	16.4
France	22.5	21.6	20.4	20.6	20.0	18.8	18.0
Germany, Fed. Rep. of	16.9	16.5	14.4	14.2	15.0	12.6	11.8
Italy	22.0	18.9	18.1	17.2	17.5	16.0	14.6
Japan	23.6	17.7	18.6	17.5	16.6	16.1	14.2
United Kingdom	21.2	19.7	18.5	18.6	19.2	16.8	16.3
United States	22.7	20.6	19.3	18.8	18.9	16.4	14.8
Average	*21.7*	*19.4*	*18.4*	*17.9*	*18.2*	*16.3*	*15.2*
Aged 15 to 64							
Canada	67.5	68.0	68.1	62.0	68.3	69.0	62.8
France	63.5	64.4	66.0	63.6	65.7	66.6	62.7
Germany, Fed. Rep. of	67.6	66.5	64.9	62.2	67.7	66.0	62.8
Italy	64.5	65.4	65.3	63.8	66.3	66.2	63.9
Japan	67.4	67.4	63.2	61.3	66.0	62.5	60.6
United Kingdom	64.0	65.2	65.7	62.9	65.3	66.4	62.9
United States	66.1	66.4	66.9	61.8	67.3	68.2	62.1
Average	*65.8*	*66.2*	*65.7*	*62.5*	*66.7*	*66.4*	*62.5*

Source: Fund staff estimates.

Table 21. Some Principal Demographic Measures, 1980–2025

(In percent, unless otherwise stated)

		Baseline Scenario			"Greater Aging" Scenario		
	1980	2000	2010	2025	2000	2010	2025
Overall dependency rate[1]							
Canada	48.1	47.0	46.8	61.3	46.4	44.9	59.2
France	57.5	55.3	51.5	57.2	51.0	50.2	59.5
Germany, Fed. Rep. of	47.9	50.4	54.1	60.8	47.7	51.5	59.2
Italy	55.0	52.8	53.1	56.7	50.8	51.1	56.4
Japan	48.4	48.4	58.1	63.2	51.5	60.0	65.0
United Kingdom	56.3	53.4	52.2	59.0	53.1	50.6	59.0
United States	51.3	50.6	49.5	61.8	48.6	46.6	61.0
Average	*52.1*	*50.9*	*52.2*	*59.8*	*49.9*	*50.7*	*59.9*
Elderly dependency rate[2]							
Canada	14.1	16.7	18.6	31.1	17.3	19.4	33.1
France	22.0	21.7	20.6	24.8	20.5	21.9	30.8
Germany, Fed. Rep. of	22.9	25.6	31.9	37.9	25.6	32.4	40.4
Italy	20.9	24.0	25.4	29.8	24.4	26.9	33.6
Japan	13.4	22.1	28.8	34.6	26.4	34.2	41.6
United Kingdom	23.1	23.2	24.0	29.4	23.7	25.3	33.1
United States	16.9	19.6	20.6	31.4	20.5	22.6	37.2
Average	*19.1*	*21.7*	*24.3*	*31.2*	*22.6*	*26.1*	*35.7*
Youth dependency rate[3]							
Canada	34.1	30.3	28.2	30.1	29.1	25.5	26.1
France	35.4	33.5	30.9	32.4	30.4	28.2	28.7
Germany, Fed Rep. of	25.0	24.8	22.2	22.8	22.2	19.1	18.8
Italy	34.1	28.9	27.7	27.0	26.4	24.2	22.8
Japan	35.0	26.3	29.4	28.6	25.2	25.8	23.4
United Kingdom	33.1	30.2	28.2	29.6	29.4	25.3	25.9
United States	34.3	31.0	28.8	30.4	28.1	24.0	23.8
Average	*33.0*	*29.2*	*27.9*	*28.7*	*27.3*	*24.6*	*24.2*
Share of the very old in the elderly population[4]							
Canada	37.9	39.5	39.4	37.8	40.7	41.0	38.5
France	40.7	40.7	47.1	36.7	43.0	43.8	42.0
Germany, Fed. Rep. of	38.7	41.2	40.1	42.4	40.5	39.7	43.3
Italy	35.6	39.5	42.8	43.7	39.5	43.3	45.1
Japan	34.4	34.9	40.1	49.5	40.2	46.3	54.4
United Kingdom	37.8	44.4	41.8	42.2	45.2	43.5	45.2
United States	40.2	50.0	47.9	43.3	50.7	50.0	45.9
Average	*37.9*	*41.5*	*42.7*	*42.2*	*42.8*	*43.9*	*44.9*
Population				*(Millions of persons)*			
Canada	24.0	29.0	30.6	32.5	29.1	30.4	31.4
France	53.6	58.2	59.8	61.3	58.3	59.8	61.4
Germany, Fed. Rep. of	61.5	58.2	57.9	53.5	58.5	55.9	49.9
Italy	56.2	58.1	58.1	57.2	57.5	57.0	54.9
Japan	116.7	128.2	131.7	131.8	131.4	133.3	127.2
United Kingdom	55.9	56.9	57.5	58.5	57.1	57.2	57.5
United States	236.4	277.5	293.9	314.1	271.9	281.7	287.9

Source: Fund staff estimates.
[1] Ratio of population aged under 15 and over 65 to population aged 15–64.
[2] Ratio of population aged 65 and over to population aged 15–64.
[3] Ratio of population aged under 15 to population aged 15–64.
[4] Ratio of population aged 75 and over to population aged 65 and over.

Table 22. Age Composition of the Population Group Aged 20–64, 1980–2025

(As percentage of population aged 20–64)

Country	1980	2000	2010	2025
Canada				
20–29	32.2	21.3	21.7	21.4
30–39	25.3	26.0	20.1	22.4
40–49	18.4	26.4	24.2	21.7
50–59	17.3	19.6	24.1	21.4
60–64	6.8	6.7	9.8	13.0
Total	*100.0*	*100.0*	*100.0*	*100.0*
France				
20–29	28.5	23.3	23.5	23.0
30–39	23.9	24.8	21.8	23.8
40–49	21.2	24.5	22.9	21.5
50–59	21.0	19.6	21.9	21.4
60–64	5.4	7.8	9.9	10.3
Total	*100.0*	*100.0*	*100.0*	*100.0*
Germany, Fed. Rep. of				
20–29	25.2	16.7	18.6	18.8
30–39	23.2	26.7	17.9	21.8
40–49	24.5	23.5	28.5	18.9
50–59	20.6	21.2	24.6	25.3
60–64	6.6	12.0	10.4	15.2
Total	*100.0*	*100.0*	*100.0*	*100.0*
Italy				
20–29	24.8	22.3	19.3	21.7
30–39	23.7	25.5	22.7	21.4
40–49	23.1	22.1	25.7	19.9
50–59	21.7	20.4	21.8	24.9
60–64	6.7	9.6	10.6	12.1
Total	*100.0*	*100.0*	*100.0*	*100.0*
Japan				
20–29	24.0	23.4	18.7	22.7
30–39	28.3	21.6	24.4	19.8
40–49	23.3	21.0	22.4	21.6
50–59	18.2	24.4	21.5	25.4
60–64	6.3	9.7	13.1	10.6
Total	*100.0*	*100.0*	*100.0*	*100.0*
United Kingdom				
20–29	25.5	21.4	20.7	21.8
30–39	24.2	26.3	21.0	22.1
40–49	20.3	22.7	25.8	20.1
50–59	21.1	21.1	21.8	23.8
60–64	9.0	8.5	10.7	12.3
Total	*100.0*	*100.0*	*100.0*	*100.0*
United States				
20–29	32.0	22.3	23.1	22.3
30–39	24.8	25.3	20.8	23.3
40–49	17.6	26.3	23.2	22.2
50–59	17.8	19.5	23.5	20.9
60–64	7.8	6.7	9.5	11.4
Total	*100.0*	*100.0*	*100.0*	*100.0*

Source: Fund staff estimates.

Table 23. Age Distribution of Government Medical Expenditure in 1980

(As percentage of total government medical expenditure)

	Share of Medical Expenditure Allocated to Age Group			Share of Population in Age Group		
Country	0–14	15–64	65 and over	0–14	15–64	65 and over
Canada	. . .	. . .	27.5	9.5	67.5	23.0
France	16.2	61.5	22.3	14.0	63.5	22.5
Germany, Fed. Rep. of	9.7	57.1	33.1	15.5	67.6	16.9
Italy[1]	8.5	49.6	41.9	17.3	60.7	22.0
Japan	9.5	64.2	26.3	9.0	67.4	23.6
United Kingdom	21.4	36.5	42.1	14.8	64.0	21.2
United States[2]	9.7	40.4	49.9	31.9	56.9	11.2

Source: Fund staff estimates.
[1] Data relate to those aged 15–59 and over 60.
[2] Data relate to those aged 0–19 and 20–64.

Table 24. Medical Expenditure and Total Government Social Expenditure, 1960–81

(As a percentage of GDP)[1]

	1960			1975			1981		
Country	Medical expen-diture	Total social expen-diture	Medical as per-centage of total	Medical expen-diture	Total social expen-diture	Medical as per-centage of total	Medical expen-diture	Total social expen-diture	Medical as per-centage of total
Canada	2.4	12.1	19.8	5.7	21.8	26.1	5.6	21.5	26.0
France	2.5	13.4[2]	18.7[2]	5.5	18.1	30.4	6.5	23.8	27.3
Germany, Fed. Rep. of	3.1	20.5	15.1	6.6	32.6	20.2	6.5	31.5	20.6
Italy	3.2	16.8	19.0	5.8	26.0	22.3	6.0	29.1	20.6
Japan	1.3	8.0	16.3	4.0	14.2	28.2	4.7	17.5	26.9
United Kingdom	3.4	13.9	24.5	5.0	22.5	22.2	5.4	23.7	22.8
United States	1.3	10.9	11.9	3.7	20.8	17.8	4.2	20.8	20.2
Average	*2.5*	*13.7*	*18.2*	*5.2*	*23.1*	*22.5*	*5.6*	*24.8*	*22.6*

Source: OECD, *Social Expenditure 1960–1990, Problems of Growth and Control* (1985).
[1] Unless otherwise stated.
[2] Excluding education.

Table 25. Some Illustrative Statistics on Medical Expenditure Per Capita by Age Group in Selected Group of Seven Countries

A. France: Index of Health Expenditure Per Capita by Age Group, 1980

(Total hospital expenditure per capita, age group 15–64 = 100)

	Public and Private				Public			
Age Group	Hospitals	Outpatient	Drugs	Total	Hospitals	Outpatient	Drugs	Total
0–14	68.8	29.6	26.7	146.5	63.7	19.4	15.1	108.4
15–64	100.0	25.0	34.7	193.0	92.5	16.3	19.6	146.0
65 and over	145.7	45.4	88.8	314.3	136.1	28.2	50.2	240.1
75 and over	194.7	49.0	102.4	384.5	180.3	31.9	57.9	298.8
Average	*99.5*	*28.6*	*39.8*	*199.4*	*92.1*	*18.6*	*22.8*	*150.6*

B. Germany (Federal Republic): Index of Health Care Expenditure Per Capita by Age Group[1]

(Expenditure on hospital care per male patient aged 15–64 = 100)

	Index of Health Care Expenditure Per Capita		Hospital Expenditure Per Capita		Outpatient Expenditure Per Capita	
Age Group	Males	Females	Males	Females	Males	Females
0–4	83.7	53.1	129.6	46.7	57.9	57.1
5–14	49.1	45.1	53.1	44.3	48.3	47.5
15–24	58.7	62.8	74.8	59.5	54.7	68.4
25–34	64.4	78.1	72.4	70.0	66.0	82.1
35–44	80.5	92.5	80.5	82.1	80.5	90.1
45–54	111.1	129.6	114.3	127.1	90.1	104.6
55–64	165.8	160.9	193.1	152.9	91.7	120.7
65–74	203.6	205.2	267.2	241.4	118.3	124.7
75 and over	259.1	257.5	391.1	371.8	132.8	137.6

[1] Derived from a 1975 Microcensus data survey and includes expenditure from a Public Health Care Fund.

C. Japan: Index of Public Expenditure on Medical Care Per Capita by Age Group, 1980[1]

(Expenditure on inpatient care, age group 15–64 = 100)

Age Group	Inpatient Care	Outpatient Care
0–14	28.9	70.4
15–44	70.7	87.7
45–64	161.2	206.8
65–69	309.3	331.1
70 and over	566.6	443.2
Average	*100.0*	*118.8*

[1] Expenditure through the Medical Insurance System.

D. United Kingdom, 1981/82: Index of Public Current Expenditure Per Capita by Age Group

(Expenditure on hospital care, age group 16–64 = 100)

Age Group	Hospital and Community Services	Family Practitioner Services	Total	Personal Social Services
0–4	176.5	58.8	235.3	70.6
5–15	82.4	47.1	129.4	76.5
16–64	100.0	52.9	152.9	17.7
65–74	382.4	76.5	458.8	76.5
75 and over	905.9	135.3	1,041.2	323.5
Average	*188.2*	*58.8*	*247.1*	*52.9*

Table 25 (*concluded*). Some Illustrative Statistics on Medical Expenditure Per Capita by Age Group in Selected Group of Seven Countries

E. United States: Index of Personal Health Care Expenditure Per Capita by Age Group, 1978

(*Total expenditure, age group 19–64 = 100*)

	Public			Private			Total		
	0–18	19–64	65 and over	0–18	19–64	65 and over	0–18	19–64	65 and over
Hospital care	6.2	19.4	99.5	7.2	29.0	14.2	13.3	48.4	113.7
Physician's care	1.6	3.4	28.4	8.3	18.0	19.5	9.8	21.5	47.9
Dentist's services	0.4	0.3	0.3	4.8	9.0	7.2	5.2	9.3	7.5
Other professional services	0.4	0.3	2.5	0.4	2.5	3.4	0.8	2.9	5.9
Drugs and drug sundries	0.3	0.6	2.7	5.0	8.5	14.7	5.3	9.2	17.4
Eyeglasses and appliances	—	0.1	1.1	0.9	2.7	2.2	0.9	2.8	3.3
Nursing home care	0.1	2.5	31.3	—	0.6	36.5	0.1	3.1	67.8
Other health services	1.7	1.9	1.7	0.2	1.0	0.2	2.0	3.0	1.9
Total	*10.7*	*28.5*	*167.5*	*26.7*	*71.4*	*97.8*	*37.4*	*100.0*	*265.2*

Sources: Nivollet (1985); Fisher (1980); United Kingdom, H.M. Treasury (1984); Kohnert (1985); Feldman (1985). See also McDonald (1985) for more recent statistics on the United States.

Table 26. Copayment and Coverage Rates in Government Medical Insurance Programs, 1960–80

	Inpatient Care		Ambulatory Care		Pharmaceuticals	
	1960	1980	1960	1980	1960	1980
Copayment rate[1]			(*As a percentage of total costs*)			
Canada	72	91	10	72	1	23
France	85	92	60	58	60	75
Germany, Fed. Rep. of	95	100	36	25	90	80
Italy	95	100	36	25	90	80
Japan	79	89	79	90	79	89
United Kingdom	90	99	92	94	87	94
United States	41	54	18	56	—	9
Coverage rate[2]			(*As a percentage of population*)			
Canada	68	100	2	100	5	33
France	85	100	85	99	85	99
Germany, Fed. Rep. of	84	91	84	91	84	91
Italy	87	100	87	100	87	100
Japan	96	100	96	100	96	100
United Kingdom	100	100	100	100	100	100
United States	22	40	6	25	6	2

Source: OECD estimates.

[1] The copayment rate equals the percentage of costs borne by the government sector where medical expenditure is under a government medical insurance program.

[2] The coverage rate equals the percentage of individuals covered by a government medical insurance program.

Table 27. Contribution of Demographic and Coverage Effects, Relative Prices, and Real Benefits to the Growth of Government Medical and Health Expenditure, 1960–81

(Annual growth rates, in percent)

	1960–75					1975–81				
Country	Demo-graphic effect	Coverage effect	Relative prices (1)	Average benefit (2)	Total (1)+(2)	Demo-graphic effect	Coverage effect	Relative prices (1)	Average benefit (2)	Total (1)+(2)
Canada	1.6	2.6	−1.4	8.4	6.9	1.2	—	—	1.8	1.8
France	1.0	1.0	−0.1	8.7	8.6	0.4	0.3	−0.7	5.6	4.9
Germany, Fed. Rep. of	1.0	0.5	2.3	5.0	7.4	—	—	0.7	2.1	2.8
Italy	0.6	0.9	2.0	5.1	7.2	0.4	0.2	3.7	−0.5	3.2
Japan	1.2	0.3	4.2	10.5	15.1	0.9	—	1.0	5.6	6.7
United Kingdom	0.4	—	1.8	3.0	4.9	—	—	0.2	2.0	2.2
United States	1.2	4.1	0.4	4.7	5.1	1.0	—	1.8	2.8	4.7
Average	*1.0*	*1.3*	*1.3*	*6.5*	*7.9*	*0.5*	*0.1*	*1.0*	*2.8*	*3.8*

Source: OECD, *Social Expenditure: 1960–1990, Problems of Growth and Control* (1985).

Table 28. OECD Estimates of the Average Growth in Real Medical Benefits Relative to the Changing Share of the Elderly, 1960–81

(In percent)

	Average Share of 65 and Over in the Population				Growth Rate of Average Real Medical Benefits	
Country	1960	1970	1975	1980	1960–75	1975–81
Canada	7.6	8.0	8.5	9.1	8.4	1.8
France	11.6	12.9	13.5	13.9	8.7	5.6
Germany, Fed. Rep. of	10.9	13.2	14.5	15.4	5.0	2.1
Italy	9.3	10.7	12.1	13.0	5.1	−0.5
Japan	6.1	7.1	7.9	8.8	10.5	5.6
United Kingdom	11.7	13.0	14.0	14.9	3.0	2.0
United States	9.2	9.8	10.5	11.2	4.7	2.8

Sources: OECD (1979); and OECD (1985).

Table 29. Number of Years of Primary and Secondary School Attendance by Years, 1980

(In years of attendance)

		Secondary			
Country	Primary	First level	Second level	Total	Of Which: Compulsory
Canada	6	3	3	12	8–10
France	5	4	3	12	10
Germany, Fed. Rep. of	4	6	3	13	9
Italy	5	3	5	13	8
Japan	6	3	3	12	9
United Kingdom	6	3	4	13	11
United States	6	3	3	12	10

Source: UNESCO, *Statistical Yearbook, 1983* (1983).

Table 30. Enrollment at Different School Levels, 1950–80

(Index: 1960 = 100, 1980 level in thousands)

	1950	1955	1960	1965	1970	1975	1980	Level 1980
Preprimary level								
Canada	50	73	100	161	248	282	282	397
France	83	95	100	133	165	194	178	2,384
Germany, Fed. Rep. of	72	85	100	120	148	206	191	1,536
Italy	81	93	100	116	137	158	159	1,841
Japan	30	87	100	153	228	309	324	2,407
United Kingdom	. . .	. . .	100	114	134	172	149	337
United States	72	88	100	126	206	246	247	5,163
Primary level								
Canada	65	83	100	113	118	77	69	2,185
France	70	89	100	95	85	79	79	4,610
Germany, Fed. Rep. of	126	96	100	109	125	126	99	5,044
Italy	103	106	100	100	108	108	99	4,435
Japan	89	97	100	78	76	82	93	11,751
United Kingdom	94	109	100	107	114	113	97	4,911
United States	72	88	100	107	96	90	92	27,448
Secondary level								
Canada	48	59	100	150	184	291	261	2,323
France	48	60	100	144	203	227	230	3,911
Germany, Fed. Rep. of	67	94	100	124	181	256	298	3,690
Italy	33	43	100	128	162	206	215	3,493
Japan	85	95	100	115	90	94	104	8,110
United Kingdom	62	74	100	99	110	136	140	5,087
United States	67	81	100	178	207	214	152	14,556
Tertiary level								
Canada	49	54	100	221	289	331	380	628
France	51	71	100	188	243	298	320	870
Germany, Fed. Rep. of	46	66	100	141	190	392	461	1,223
Italy	. . .	. . .	100	116	195	277	317	1,111
Japan	55	77	100	153	212	259	273	1,937
United Kingdom	. . .	. . .	100	137	190	254	299	408
United States	64	74	100	154	176	202	211	7,573
Overall enrollment								
Canada	60	77	100	126	142	137	127	5,533
France	67	84	100	112	123	130	129	11,775
Germany, Fed. Rep. of	107	93	100	114	139	166	156	11,494
Italy	. . .	. . .	100	109	128	144	143	10,879
Japan	84	96	100	96	91	99	111	24,205
United Kingdom	. . .	. . .	100	104	114	126	118	10,742
United States	71	86	100	126	131	132	121	54,740

Source: UNESCO, *Statistical Yearbook, 1983* (1983).

Table 31. School Enrollment Rates, 1960–80

(Enrollment as percentage of relevant age groups)

	1960	1965	1970	1975	1980
Secondary level					
Canada (12–17)	46	56	65	92	89
France (11–17)	46	56	74	82	85
Germany, Fed. Rep. of (6–18)	69	71	78	82	80
Italy (11–18)	34	47	61	72	73
Japan (12–17)	74	82	86	92	93
United Kingdom (11–17)	66	66	73	82	83
United States (13–17)	100	100	100	100	100
Tertiary level					
Canada (20–24)	16	26	35	39	36
France (20–24)	10	18	20	24	26
Germany, Fed. Rep. of (20–24)	6	9	13	25	28
Italy (20–24)	7	11	17	26	27
Japan (20–24)	9	13	17	25	30
United Kingdom (20–24)	9	12	14	19	20
United States (20–24)	32	40	49	58	57

Source: UNESCO, *Statistical Yearbook, 1983* (1983).

Table 32. Public Expenditure per Student by Level of Education, 1980

	In U.S. Dollars Converted at:		As a Percentage of:	
	Purchasing power parity rate	Market exchange rate	Per capita income	Average production worker wage
Primary education				
Canada[1]	2,253	2,253	21.7	16.2
France	937	1,020	8.9	8.8
Germany, Fed. Rep. of	1,556	1,787	14.5	11.2
Italy	1,011	821	12.9	8.7
Japan	1,793	2,138	21.5	17.4
United Kingdom	1,405	1,579	16.3	12.0
United States[1]	1,522	1,522	13.2	10.1
Secondary education				
Canada[1]	2,253	2,253	21.7	16.2
France	2,603	2,833	24.7	24.5
Germany, Fed. Rep. of	1,690	1,940	15.7	12.1
Italy	1,208	981	15.4	10.4
Japan	1,921	2,291	23.0	18.6
United Kingdom	1,405	1,579	16.3	12.0
United States[1]	1,522	1,522	13.2	10.1
Tertiary education				
Canada	5,300	5,300	51.0	38.2
France	3,918	4,265	37.2	36.9
Germany, Fed. Rep. of	6,509	7,473	60.7	46.8
Italy	1,208	981	15.4	10.4
Japan	3,143	3,747	37.7	30.4
United Kingdom	5,375	6,041	62.3	46.1
United States	3,479	3,479	30.1	23.2

Source: Fund staff estimates.
[1] Reflects average of primary and secondary levels.

Appendix II

Summary of Major Public Pension Programs and Their Average Benefits

Summary of Major Public Pension Programs

Canada

Old Age Security

This universal scheme pays a flat-rate pension to all residents aged 65 and over. Forty years of residence is required for a full pension. A Guaranteed Income Supplement, based upon income in the previous year, which is reduced by Can$1.00 a month for every Can$2.00 of other income, and an income-tested spouse allowance are also paid. Benefits are increased in line with consumer prices. The scheme is financed by general revenue.

Canada and Quebec Pension Plans

These are compulsory social insurance schemes that provide earnings-related pensions for employees and the self-employed. The retirement pension is equal to 25 percent of average contributory career earnings, above a minimum and up to a maximum. There is a low-earnings disregard. Pension age is 65. Disability pensions, survivor pensions, and a lump-sum death benefit are provided. Pensions are increased in line with consumer prices. The schemes are financed through contributions made by employees and employers on earnings between the minimum and maximum applied in determining benefits.

France

Basic Scheme (Régime général)

This social insurance scheme provides earnings-related pensions for wage earners. Pension age is 60, with a full pension requiring contributions for 37.5 years. The retirement pension is equal to 50 percent of average earnings in the ten highest years. Past earnings are revalued to reflect wage growth. There is an income-tested spouse supplement. Disability and survivor pensions are provided. Pensions are increased in line with average wages. The scheme is financed through earnings-related contributions made by employees and employers. There is a maximum earnings level for both benefit and contribution purposes.

Special Schemes

There are compulsory schemes for agricultural workers, seamen, railway employees, public utility and other public employees, and the self-employed. The schemes provide earnings-related retirement pensions, with the benefit formula varying between schemes. Many pensioners receive more than one pension. Pension age varies between 60 and 65, depending upon the scheme. Disability and survivor pensions are also provided. Finance is provided by employees, employers, and general revenue.

Germany, Federal Republic of

Old Age, Survivors', and Disability Insurance

An employee becomes eligible to receive retirement pension benefits at age 65 if he or she has been in the scheme for five years, and at age 63 with 35 years in the scheme. Under certain conditions, women, disabled persons, and the unemployed receive a retirement pension at age 60. The retirement pension and the general disability pension are equal to 1.5 percent of "assessed" wages for each year in the scheme. The pension rate is reduced to 1 percent of assessed wages for each year in the scheme in the case of occupational disability pensions. "Assessed" wages have been revalued to reflect wage growth. Pensions have been increased in the past to reflect the growth in gross wages, although in recent years this link has been broken, and pensions are now in fact indexed to net wages. The scheme is financed through earnings-related employee and employer contributions, and a general government subsidy. There are minimum and maximum earnings levels for both benefit and contribution purposes.

Public Sector Employees' Pension Scheme

This scheme pays a retirement pension of 75 percent of pensionable income to civil servants with over 35 years of coverage. The scheme is financed by general revenue. Other public sector employees receive pensions from the social insurance scheme, but they are brought up to a comparable level through additional pension schemes for public employees paid for by employers. Disability and survivor pensions are provided.

Italy

General Scheme (FPLD)

This social insurance scheme provides earnings-related pensions for employees in industry and commerce. The retirement pension is equal to 2 percent of the average of the last five years' earnings for each year of scheme membership, up to a maximum of 80 percent of earnings, which are themselves subject to a maximum. Pension age is 60 for men and 55 for women with 15 years of coverage. A means-tested old-age benefit is available to those with very low pensions. Disability and survivor pensions are paid. Pensions are increased in line with a composite index reflecting changes in the cost of living and wages. The scheme is financed through earnings-related employee and employer contributions, subject to a minimum, and a lump-sum government subsidy.

Special Schemes

There is a large number (over 50) of similar schemes for those not covered by the general scheme. Multiple pensions are common.

Japan

Employees Pension Insurance (Koosei)

This is part of a dual social insurance scheme that provides earnings-related pensions for employees. The retirement pension is equal to a fixed amount for each year of coverage, up to a maximum of 35, plus 1 percent of average revalued lifetime earnings. Pension age is 60 for men and 55 for women with 20 years in the scheme. Disability and survivor pensions are provided. Pensions are automatically adjusted to reflect changes in the cost of living. The scheme is financed by earnings-related contributions charged to employees and employers, subject to a minimum and a maximum, and 20 percent of the cost of the scheme is met by the Government of Japan.

National Pension Program (Kokumin)

This second part of a dual social insurance scheme provides pensions for residents not covered by another scheme. The retirement pension is equal to a fixed amount per year of contribution. Pension age is 65, a reduced pension being paid in the event of earlier retirement. Disability and survivor pensions are provided. Pensions are automatically adjusted to reflect changes in the cost of living. Individuals pay a fixed contribution, and one third of the cost of the scheme is met by the Government of Japan.

Other Programs

There are eight programs providing pensions for central and local government employees, other public sector employees, and agricultural workers, as well as a program providing worker disability insurance.

1985 Pension Reform Act

A basic benefit, common to all programs, has been introduced. Pension age is to be 65, but as an interim measure, basic benefits will be paid from age 60. Employees' earnings-related pensions are to be limited to 68 percent of average revalued lifetime earnings. Without the reform, replacement rates would have risen to 83 percent. All replacement rates will reach 68 percent by 2010. In addition, pension provision for women and disabled people has been improved.

United Kingdom

State Earnings-Related Pension Scheme (SERPS)

This social insurance scheme provides pensions for employees and the self-employed. The retirement pension consists of a basic flat-rate component, plus an earnings-related component equal to 1.25 percent of average revalued earnings in the best 20 years of a working life, beginning in April 1978. An earnings index is used for revaluation. There is an income-tested allowance for needy pensioners. Pension age is 65 for men and 60 for women. Disability and survivor pensions are provided. Pensions are adjusted to reflect price changes. The scheme is financed by earnings-related contributions paid by employees and employers and by a government contribution. A minimum and a maximum earnings level applies in the determination of both contributions and benefits. Employers can contract out of the earnings-related component if they provide similar pensions through a private scheme.

Graduated Pensions

This scheme began in April 1961 and was wound up in March 1975. It pays small amounts of pension based upon earnings-related contributions made over this period.

1985 White Paper

SERPS is to be reformed in the following ways: earnings-related pensions are to be limited to 20 percent of average revalued lifetime earnings; pension provision for widows and widowers has been reduced; and contracting-out terms have been changed.

United States

Old Age, Survivors', and Disability Insurance (OASDI)

This social insurance scheme provides pensions for most gainfully occupied persons. The retirement pension is based on covered earnings after 1950, with a low earnings disregard. The pension formula has undergone change, the intention being to bring about a phased reduction in the replacement rate from its 1981 peak average of 54 percent to 45 percent by 1990. A dependent's allowance is paid, as well as a means-tested allowance for the needy. Pension age is 65. Retirement age is to be increased from 65 to 67 between 2000 and 2025. Pensions are increased in line with the cost of living. The scheme is financed through earnings-related contributions paid by employees, a payroll tax, and a government contribution. There is a maximum earnings level for pension purposes.

Other Schemes

There are separate programs for federal government and military employees, and for veterans. There is also a Supplementary Security Income program to help those with very low incomes.

Average Benefit Levels

Table 33 provides estimates on the average payment under the various public pension schemes prevailing in the seven major industrial countries as of 1980. Given the variety of benefits and the different scales at which they are paid, reliance has been placed on a measure of average expenditures, either per pension recipient or per person over age 65. Such comparisons are crude, as systems differ in the comprehensiveness of benefits paid to different classes of beneficiaries (the retired, spouses of retirees, survivors' benefits to widows and dependent children, the disabled, veterans, early retirees), as to whether such benefits are taxable, and in the relative weight of income-related and flat-rate benefits. The average is also affected by the number of recipients in the different groups.

These averages have been stated both in terms of U.S. dollars (using both the current exchange rate and the purchasing power parity rate[71]) and relative to the average wage of a production worker (APW) and to the per capita income prevailing in 1980. The higher relative ratio of pension expenditure to GDP in France, the Federal Republic of Germany, and Italy in part appears to be influenced by the higher average pension benefits prevailing in these countries. This is clearly the case in France and the Federal Republic of Germany. In Italy, the average pension in any given program is not any larger than in the other countries, but multiple pensions per recipient appear to characterize the Italian social insurance system. The average pension expenditure per citizen over age 60 is substantially higher than the average pension in any given scheme; while the former number undoubtedly overestimates the average pension actually received by individuals over age 60 (to the extent that some expenditures go to dependents or individuals below that age), it offers a better measure of the actual pension level. The level of pensions in these three countries also reflects their greater reliance on public pension schemes as a source of income support for the elderly.

Canada, the United Kingdom, and the United States are in the next strata in terms of average pension benefits per recipient, relative to per capita income or the wage of an average production worker. Japan appears to have the lowest average pension expenditures within this group of countries because of the recent introduction and relative immaturity of Japan's pension systems.[72] Private pensions do not play as important a role, although many permanent employees still receive (though in diminishing numbers) a lump-sum payment at the time of retirement. The elderly in Japan appear to rely principally on continued employment, savings, or family support.

---

[71] Exchange rates in 1975 are adjusted to 1980, based on relative movements in the consumer price index between a given country and the United States.

[72] However, for the hypothetical worker enrolled for an average working life at average wages, the benefits under the Japanese system would be comparable to those received by a hypothetical average worker in other industrial countries.